Stimmt!

Edexcel GCSE (9–1) German
Foundation
Vocabulary Book

Pearson

Published by Pearson Education Limited, 80 Strand, London, WC2R 0RL
www.pearsonschoolsandfecolleges.co.uk
Text © Pearson Education Limited 2017
Editorial management by Gwladys Rushworth for Haremi
Edited by Anne Urbschat
Typeset by York Publishing Solutions Pvt. Ltd.
Cover image: Shutterstock.com: Bildagentur Zoonar GmbH
Cover © Pearson Education Limited 2017

Written by Melissa Weir

First published 2017
10 9 8

British Library Cataloguing in Publication Data
A catalogue record for this book is available from the British Library.
ISBN 978 1 292 17255 2

Copyright notice
All rights reserved. No part of this publication may be reproduced in any form or by any means (including photocopying or storing it in any medium by electronic means and whether or not transiently or incidentally to some other use of this publication) without the written permission of the copyright owner, except in accordance with the provisions of the Copyright, Design and Patents Act 1988 or under the terms of a license issued by the Copyright Licensing Agency, Barnard's Inn, 86 Fetter Lane, London EC4A 1EN (www.cla.co.uk). Applications for the copyright owner's written permission should be addressed to the publisher.

Printed in the UK by Ashford Colour Press

Inhalt

High-frequency words 4

Kapitel 1
Words I should know for speaking and writing activities 13
Extra words I should know for reading and listening activities 16

Kapitel 2
Words I should know for speaking and writing activities 18
Extra words I should know for reading and listening activities 20

Kapitel 3
Words I should know for speaking and writing activities 21
Extra words I should know for reading and listening activities 24

Kapitel 4
Words I should know for speaking and writing activities 26
Extra words I should know for reading and listening activities 29

Kapitel 5
Words I should know for speaking and writing activities 30
Extra words I should know for reading and listening activities 33

Kapitel 6
Words I should know for speaking and writing activities 34
Extra words I should know for reading and listening activities 37

Kapitel 7
Words I should know for speaking and writing activities 38
Extra words I should know for reading and listening activities 41

Kapitel 8
Words I should know for speaking and writing activities 42
Extra words I should know for reading and listening activities 45

High-frequency words

Common verbs

abfahren	to depart
ankommen	to arrive
sich beeilen	to hurry
besuchen	to visit
bleiben	to stay
eintreten	to enter
fahren	to drive
fallen	to fall
hineingehen	to enter
sich hinsetzen	to sit down
kommen	to come
laufen	to walk, to run
einen Spaziergang machen	to go for a walk
spazieren	to walk
springen	to jump
steigen	to climb, to get on
verlassen	to leave (a place)
vorbeigehen	to pass by
zurückfahren	to return
zurückgehen	to return
zurückkehren	to return
zurückkommen	to come back

Had a look ☐ **Nearly there** ☐ **Nailed it** ☐

begleiten	to accompany
bringen	to bring, to take
fliehen	to escape
folgen	to follow
führen	to lead
landen	to land
fallen lassen	to drop
leben	to live (to be alive)
nehmen	to take
parken	to park
schlafen	to sleep
sterben	to die
stoppen	to stop
warten auf	to wait for
wohnen	to live (in a)
lassen	to leave
legen	to lay
liegen	to lie
sitzen	to sit
werfen	to throw

Had a look ☐ **Nearly there** ☐ **Nailed it** ☐

aufmachen	to open
sich befinden	to be located
begegnen	to meet
berühren	to touch
drücken	to push
halten	to stop, to hold
holen	to fetch
kleben	to stick, to glue
klopfen	to knock
laden	to load, to charge
öffnen	to open
schlagen	to knock, to hit
schließen	to shut
stecken	to put
stellen	to put
tragen	to wear, to carry
zumachen	to close, to shut
zurückstellen	to put back

Had a look ☐ **Nearly there** ☐ **Nailed it** ☐

sich amüsieren	to enjoy oneself
arbeiten	to work
ausleihen	to lend
einladen	to invite
einschlafen	to fall asleep
essen	to eat
fressen	to eat (animal)
fernsehen	to watch television
forschen	to research
klettern	to climb
sich kümmern um	to look after
sich langweilen	to be bored
lernen	to learn
lesen	to read
schenken	to give (presents)
studieren	to study (at university)
im Internet surfen	to surf the internet
(sich) treffen	to meet
trinken	to drink
verbringen	to spend (time)

Had a look ☐ **Nearly there** ☐ **Nailed it** ☐

sich ärgern	to be annoyed
bedauern	to regret
sich erinnern (an)	to remember
fühlen	to feel
gehören	to belong
helfen	to help
lächeln	to smile
lachen	to laugh
leid tun	to be sorry
lieben	to love
lügen	to tell a lie
meinen	to think, to say
(sich) streiten	to argue
vergeben	to forgive
vergessen	to forget
vermissen	to miss

High-frequency words

verpassen	*to miss*	anfangen	*to begin*
versprechen	*to promise*	aufhören	*to stop*
verzeihen	*to forgive*	beenden	*to end*
weinen	*to cry*	beginnen	*to begin*
wissen	*to know*	dauern	*to last*
wünschen	*to wish*	enden	*to finish, to end*

Had a look ☐ **Nearly there** ☐ **Nailed it** ☐

		erreichen	*to reach*
		geschehen	*to happen*
anrufen	*to phone*	gewinnen	*to win*
antworten	*to answer*	nachsehen	*to check*
beantworten	*to answer*	notieren	*to note*
beschreiben	*to describe*	organisieren	*to organise*
besprechen	*to discuss*	passieren	*to happen*
sich bewerben um	*to apply for*	planen	*to plan*
denken	*to think*	produzieren	*to produce*
diskutieren	*to discuss*	scheitern	*to fail*
erklären	*to explain*	schiefgehen	*to go wrong*
erzählen	*to tell*	verbessern	*to improve*
fragen	*to ask*	verlieren	*to lose*
informieren	*to inform*	versuchen	*to try*
mitteilen	*to inform*	vorstellen	*to introduce*

Had a look ☐ **Nearly there** ☐ **Nailed it** ☐

plaudern	*to chat*		
reden	*to talk*	bedienen	*to serve*
sagen	*to say*	befehlen	*to order (command)*
schreiben	*to write*	benutzen	*to use*
sprechen	*to speak*	beraten	*to advise*
eine Frage stellen	*to ask a question*	bestellen	*to order (food)*
telefonieren (mit)	*to phone*	bitten um	*to ask for*
tippen	*to type*	danken	*to thank*
unterschreiben	*to sign*	empfehlen	*to recommend*
wiederholen	*to repeat*	füllen	*to fill*
zuhören	*to listen*	geben	*to give*

Had a look ☐ **Nearly there** ☐ **Nailed it** ☐

		gelingen	*to succeed*
		raten	*to advise*
annehmen	*to accept*	reparieren	*to repair*
bekommen	*to receive*	reservieren	*to reserve*
beschließen	*to decide*	retten	*to save, to rescue*
bevorzugen	*to prefer*	schicken	*to send*
brauchen	*to need*	wechseln	*to change*

Had a look ☐ **Nearly there** ☐ **Nailed it** ☐

sich entscheiden	*to decide*		
erhalten	*to receive*	finden	*to find*
erlauben	*to allow*	glauben	*to believe, to think*
erwarten	*to expect*	haben	*to have*
fehlen	*to be missing*	heißen	*to be called*
sich freuen auf	*to look forward to*	hoffen	*to hope*
gefallen	*to please*	hören	*to hear*
gern haben	*to like*	kennen	*to know (be familiar with)*
hassen	*to hate*	nennen	*to name*
sich interessieren für	*to be interested in*	schauen	*to look*
verhindern	*to prevent*	scheinen	*to seem, to shine*
vermeiden	*to avoid*	sehen	*to see*
vorhaben	*to intend*	verstehen	*to understand*
werden	*to become*	wählen	*to choose, to dial*

Had a look ☐ **Nearly there** ☐ **Nailed it** ☐

High-frequency words

zeigen	*to show*
dürfen	*to be allowed to*
können	*to be able to*
mögen	*to like*
müssen	*to have to*
sollen	*to be supposed to*
wollen	*to want*
zusehen	*to look, to watch*

Had a look ☐ **Nearly there** ☐ **Nailed it** ☐

ausgeben	*to spend (money)*
einkaufen	*to shop*
einschalten	*to light, to turn on*
kaufen	*to buy*
klicken	*to click*
klingeln	*to ring*
kosten	*to cost*
leihen	*to borrow, to hire*
mieten	*to rent, to hire*
schneien	*to snow*
schweigen	*to be silent*
stehlen	*to steal*
verdienen	*to earn*
verkaufen	*to sell*
zahlen	*to pay*
zählen	*to count*

Had a look ☐ **Nearly there** ☐ **Nailed it** ☐

Common adjectives

ärgerlich	*annoying*
böse	*angry*
dumm	*stupid*
eilig	*in a hurry*
ermüdend	*tiring*
ernst	*serious*
erschöpft	*exhausted*
faul	*lazy*
launisch	*moody*
laut	*loud, noisy*
müde	*tired*
schüchtern	*shy*
schwach	*weak*
schwer	*heavy, serious*
streng	*strict*
traurig	*sad*
zornig	*angry*

Had a look ☐ **Nearly there** ☐ **Nailed it** ☐

artig	*well-behaved*
brav	*well-behaved*
beschäftigt	*busy*
dankbar	*grateful*
dynamisch	*dynamic*
fleißig	*hard-working*

geduldig	*patient*
gesund	*healthy*
glücklich	*happy*
gut gelaunt	*in a good mood*
komisch	*funny, comical*
lustig	*funny*
nett	*kind, nice*
reif	*mature, ripe*
reizend	*charming*
schnell	*fast, quick*
stark	*strong*
stolz	*proud*
verantwortlich	*responsible*
zufrieden	*satisfied*

Had a look ☐ **Nearly there** ☐ **Nailed it** ☐

groß	*big, tall*
klein	*little, small*
lang	*long*
kurz	*short*
hoch	*high*
niedrig	*low*
breit	*broad*
schmal	*slim, narrow*
dicht	*dense*
eng	*narrow, tight*
dünn	*thin*
rund	*round*
steil	*steep*
nah	*near*
weit	*far*
voll	*full*
leer	*empty*
erst–	*first*
letzt–	*last*
nächst–	*next*

Had a look ☐ **Nearly there** ☐ **Nailed it** ☐

alt	*old*
jung	*young*
jünger	*younger*
dick	*fat*
schlank	*slim*
hübsch	*pretty*
schön	*beautiful*
hässlich	*ugly*
krank	*ill*
reich	*rich*
satt	*full*

Had a look ☐ **Nearly there** ☐ **Nailed it** ☐

gut	*good*
ausgezeichnet	*excellent*
fantastisch	*fantastic*

High-frequency words

großartig	magnificent
klasse	sensational
perfekt	perfect
prima	marvellous
toll	great
wunderbar	wonderful
Lieblings-	favourite
aufregend	exciting
spannend	exciting, tense
ekelhaft	disgusting
enttäuscht	disappointed
langweilig	boring
schlecht	bad
schrecklich	awful, terrible

Had a look ☐ **Nearly there** ☐ **Nailed it** ☐

bequem	comfortable
dreckig	dirty
flexibel	flexible
gebrochen	broken
gefährlich	dangerous
geöffnet	open
geschlossen	closed
heiß	hot
kaputt	broken
kostenlos	free (of charge)
neu	new
nötig	necessary
notwendig	necessary
offen	open
sauber	clean
schmutzig	dirty
teuer	expensive
umweltfeindlich	environmentally damaging
umweltfreundlich	environmentally friendly
weich	soft
zerbrochen	broken

Had a look ☐ **Nearly there** ☐ **Nailed it** ☐

allgemein	general
bestimmt	definite
echt	real(ly)
wahr	true
richtig	correct, right
falsch	false
aktuell	current
ehemalig	old, former
genau	exact
gleich	same
gültig	valid
klar	clear
möglich	possible
nützlich	useful
typisch	typical
unterschiedlich	variable
wertvoll	valuable
wichtig	important
wirklich	real(ly)
zahlreich	numerous

Had a look ☐ **Nearly there** ☐ **Nailed it** ☐

alle	all
eigen	own
ander–	other
einzig	only
allein	alone
zusammen	together
leise	quiet
lautlos	soundless, silent
friedlich	peaceful
ruhig	calm
frei	free, vacant
bereit	ready
fertig	ready
leicht	easy, light
schwierig	difficult
schwer	hard, heavy, difficult
erstaunlich	astonishing
unglaublich	unbelievable
unvorstellbar	unimaginable
erfreut	pleased
erstaunt	astonished
überrascht	surprised

Had a look ☐ **Nearly there** ☐ **Nailed it** ☐

Common adverbs

oben	above, upstairs
unten	below, downstairs
vorwärts	forwards
rückwärts	backwards
hier	here
da	there
dort	there
da drüben	over there
irgendwo	somewhere
draußen	outside
mitten (in / auf / an / ...)	in the middle of
unterwegs	en route, on the way
immer	always
oft	often
regelmäßig	regularly
manchmal	sometimes
kaum	barely, hardly
nie	never
neulich	recently
sofort	immediately, straight away

Had a look ☐ **Nearly there** ☐ **Nailed it** ☐

High-frequency words

besonders	*especially*
sehr	*very*
wirklich	*really*
ziemlich	*rather, quite*
zu	*too*
immer noch	*still*
fast	*almost*
genug	*enough*
jedoch	*however*
leider	*unfortunately*
vielleicht	*perhaps*
wahrscheinlich	*probably*
besser	*better*
gern	*willingly*
lieber	*rather (preferably)*
mehr	*more*
nur	*only*
schon	*already*
langsam	*slowly*
schnell	*quickly*

Had a look ☐ **Nearly there** ☐ **Nailed it** ☐

Prepositions

bis	*until*
durch	*through*
entlang	*along*
für	*for*
gegen	*against*
ohne	*without*
um	*around*
wider	*against*

Had a look ☐ **Nearly there** ☐ **Nailed it** ☐

aus	*out of*
außer	*except*
bei	*at, with, next to*
gegenüber	*opposite*
mit	*with*
nach	*after*
seit	*since*
von	*from*
zu	*to*
hin zu	*towards*

Had a look ☐ **Nearly there** ☐ **Nailed it** ☐

an	*at*
auf	*on*
hinter	*behind*
in	*in, into*
neben	*next to*
über	*above, over*
unter	*beneath, under*
vor	*in front of*
zwischen	*between*

Had a look ☐ **Nearly there** ☐ **Nailed it** ☐

statt	*instead of*
trotz	*despite*
während	*during*
wegen	*because of*

Had a look ☐ **Nearly there** ☐ **Nailed it** ☐

Colours

die Farbe	*colour*
blau	*blue*
braun	*brown*
dunkel	*dark*
gelb	*yellow*
grau	*grey*
grün	*green*
hell	*light*
lila	*violet*
rosa	*pink*
rot	*red*
schwarz	*black*
weiß	*white*

Had a look ☐ **Nearly there** ☐ **Nailed it** ☐

Numbers

eins	*one (1)*
zwei	*two (2)*
drei	*three (3)*
vier	*four (4)*
fünf	*five (5)*
sechs	*six (6)*
sieben	*seven (7)*
acht	*eight (8)*
neun	*nine (9)*
zehn	*ten (10)*
elf	*eleven (11)*
zwölf	*twelve (12)*
dreizehn	*thirteen (13)*
vierzehn	*fourteen (14)*
fünfzehn	*fifteen (15)*
sechzehn	*sixteen (16)*
siebzehn	*seventeen (17)*
achtzehn	*eighteen (18)*
neunzehn	*nineteen (19)*
zwanzig	*twenty (20)*

Had a look ☐ **Nearly there** ☐ **Nailed it** ☐

einundzwanzig	*twenty-one (21)*
zweiundzwanzig	*twenty-two (22)*
dreiundzwanzig	*twenty-three (23)*
vierundzwanzig	*twenty-four (24)*
fünfundzwanzig	*twenty-five (25)*
sechsundzwanzig	*twenty-six (26)*
siebenundzwanzig	*twenty-seven (27)*
achtundzwanzig	*twenty-eight (28)*

High-frequency words

neunundzwanzig	twenty-nine (29)
dreißig	thirty (30)

Had a look ☐ Nearly there ☐ Nailed it ☐

vierzig	forty (40)
fünfzig	fifty (50)
sechzig	sixty (60)
siebzig	seventy (70)
achtzig	eighty (80)
neunzig	ninety (90)
hundert	(one) hundred (100)
einhundert	(one) hundred (100)
hunderteins	one hundred and one (101)
hundertzwanzig	one hundred and twenty (120)
zweihundert	two hundred (200)
tausend	one thousand (1,000)
eintausend	one thousand (1,000)
tausendeinhundert	one thousand one hundred (1,100)
elfhundert	one thousand one hundred (1,100)
zweitausend	two thousand (2,000)
(eine) Million	one million (1,000,000)
zwei Millionen	two million (2,000,000)

Had a look ☐ Nearly there ☐ Nailed it ☐

erster/erste/erstes	first
zweiter/zweite/zweites	second
elfter/elfte/elftes	eleventh
einundzwanzigster/ einundzwanzigste/ einundzwanzigstes	twenty-first

Had a look ☐ Nearly there ☐ Nailed it ☐

Quantities and measures

viele	many
mehrere	several
genug	enough
ein bisschen	a little
ein Drittel	a third (of)
ein Dutzend	a dozen
eine Dose	a tin (of)
eine Flasche	a bottle (of)
ein Glas	a jar (of)
eine Kiste	a box (of)
eine Packung	a packet (of)
eine Schachtel	a box (of)
eine Scheibe	a slice (of)
ein Stück	a piece (of)
eine Tafel	a bar (of)
eine Tüte	a bag (of)

Had a look ☐ Nearly there ☐ Nailed it ☐

Some useful connecting words

aber	but
also	so
anstatt	instead
auch	also
außerdem	additionally, moreover
dafür	instead
danach	afterwards
dann	then
deshalb	for this reason
deswegen	for this reason
jedoch	however
nachher	afterwards, later
oder	or
übrigens	by the way, moreover
und	and
vorher	beforehand
weil	because
zuerst	first of all

Had a look ☐ Nearly there ☐ Nailed it ☐

Time expressions

der Tag(e)	day
der Morgen(–)	morning
der Vormittag(e)	morning
der Nachmittag(e)	afternoon
der Abend(e)	evening
die Nacht (Nächte)	night
Mitternacht	midnight
die Woche(n)	week
das Wochenende(n)	weekend
gestern	yesterday
heute	today
morgen	tomorrow
morgen früh	tomorrow morning
übermorgen	the day after tomorrow
vorgestern	the day before yesterday
die Minute(n)	minute

Had a look ☐ Nearly there ☐ Nailed it ☐

ab	from
ab und zu	now and then
von Zeit zu Zeit	from time to time
am Anfang	at the start
bald	soon
früh	early
heutzutage	nowadays
immer	always
immer noch	still
jetzt	now
meistens	mostly
nächst–	next
pünktlich	on time
rechtzeitig	on time

High-frequency words

seit	since
sofort	immediately
spät	late
später	later
täglich	every day, daily
wöchentlich	weekly

Had a look ☐ Nearly there ☐ Nailed it ☐

Times of day

(um) ein Uhr	(at) one o'clock
13.00 Uhr	one o'clock (1 p.m.)
dreizehn Uhr	one o'clock (1 p.m.)
21.00 Uhr	nine o'clock (9 p.m.)
einundzwanzig Uhr	nine o'clock (9 p.m.)
neun Uhr abends	nine o'clock in the evening
genau um 14.00 Uhr	at exactly two o'clock (2 p.m.)
genau um vierzehn Uhr	at exactly two o'clock (2 p.m.)
gegen … Uhr	at about … o'clock
ungefähr um … Uhr	at about … o'clock
es ist 3.05 Uhr	it is five past three
es ist drei Uhr fünf	it is five past three
fünf vor drei	five to three
zehn nach vier	ten past four
zehn vor vier	ten to four
Viertel vor sechs	quarter to six
Viertel nach sieben	quarter past seven
halb elf	half past ten

Had a look ☐ Nearly there ☐ Nailed it ☐

Days of the week

Montag	Monday
Dienstag	Tuesday
Mittwoch	Wednesday
Donnerstag	Thursday
Freitag	Friday
Samstag	Saturday
Sonnabend	Saturday
Sonntag	Sunday
(am) Montag	(on) Monday
(am) Montagvormittag	(on) Monday morning
(am) Montagabend	(on) Monday evening
montags	on Mondays
jeden Montag	every Monday

Had a look ☐ Nearly there ☐ Nailed it ☐

Months and seasons

der Monat(e)	month
Januar	January
Februar	February
März	March
April	April
Mai	May
Juni	June
Juli	July
August	August
September	September
Oktober	October
November	November
Dezember	December
die Jahreszeit(en)	season
(im) Frühling	(in) spring
(im) Sommer	(in) summer
(im) Herbst	(in) autumn
(im) Winter	(in) winter

Had a look ☐ Nearly there ☐ Nailed it ☐

Question words

wann?	when?
warum?	why?
was für?	what sort of?
was?	what?
wen? wem?	whom?
wer?	who?, whom?
wessen?	whose?
wie viel(e)?	how much?, how many?
wie?	how?
wo?	where?

Had a look ☐ Nearly there ☐ Nailed it ☐

Other useful expressions

Es gibt …	There is/are …
Hier gibt es …	Here is/are …
Man darf nicht …	You are not allowed to …
Man muss …	You/one must …
Wie schreibt man das?	How do you spell that?
Was bedeutet das?	What does that mean?
Noch einmal?	Once again?
Ich verstehe nicht.	I don't understand.
Ich weiß es nicht.	I don't know.
Es geht mir gut.	I'm fine.
Ich bin satt.	I'm full. / I've had enough (to eat).
Natürlich!	Of course!
In Ordnung!	OK! (in agreement)
Mit Vergnügen!	With pleasure!
Viel Glück!	Good luck!
Schade!	Too bad! / What a shame!
Genug davon!	That's enough!

Had a look ☐ Nearly there ☐ Nailed it ☐

Opinions

Meiner Meinung nach …	In my opinion …
Ich denke, dass …	In my opinion …
Persönlich …	Personally, …
Das interessiert mich nicht.	That doesn't interest me / appeal to me.
Es ärgert mich.	It annoys me.

High-frequency words

Es bringt mich zum Lachen.	*It makes me laugh.*	die Schweiz	*Switzerland*
Es gefällt mir.	*I like it.*	Schottland	*Scotland*
Es ist mir egal.	*I don't mind.*	Spanien	*Spain*
Es kommt darauf an.	*It depends.*	die Türkei	*Turkey*
Es lohnt sich nicht.	*It's not worth it.*	die USA	*the United States*
Es macht nichts.	*It doesn't matter.*	die Vereinigten Staaten	*the United States*
		Wales	*Wales*

Had a look ☐ **Nearly there** ☐ **Nailed it** ☐   **Had a look** ☐ **Nearly there** ☐ **Nailed it** ☐

Other useful words

ja	*yes*
nein	*no*
das	*that*
etwas	*something*
ob	*whether, if*
wenn	*if, when*
wie	*as, like*
alle	*everyone*
jeder	*everybody*
jemand	*someone*
zum Beispiel	*for example*

Had a look ☐ **Nearly there** ☐ **Nailed it** ☐

das Ding(e)	*thing*
die Sache(n)	*thing*
der Gegenstand (-stände)	*object*
die Form(en)	*shape*
die Art(en)	*type*
die Weise(n)	*way*
die Nummer(n)	*number*
das Mal(e)	*time*
die Zahl(en)	*figure, number*
die Mitte(n)	*middle*
das Ende(n)	*end*
Herr ...	*Mr ...*
Frau ...	*Mrs ...*

Had a look ☐ **Nearly there** ☐ **Nailed it** ☐

Countries

Belgien	*Belgium*
Dänemark	*Denmark*
Deutschland	*Germany*
England	*England*
Frankreich	*France*
Griechenland	*Greece*
Großbritannien	*Great Britain*
Indien	*India*
Irland	*Ireland*
Italien	*Italy*
die Niederlande	*the Netherlands*
Österreich	*Austria*
Polen	*Poland*
Russland	*Russia*

Continents

Afrika	*Africa*
Asien	*Asia*
Australien	*Australia*
Europa	*Europe*
Nordamerika	*North America*
Südamerika	*South America*

Had a look ☐ **Nearly there** ☐ **Nailed it** ☐

Nationalities

Amerikaner(in)	*American*
amerikanisch	*American*
Belgier(in)	*Belgian*
belgisch	*Belgian*
Brite/Britin	*British*
britisch	*British*
Däne/Dänin	*Danish*
dänisch	*Danish*
Deutsche(r)	*German*
deutsch	*German*
Engländer(in)	*English*
englisch	*English*
Franzose/Französin	*French*
französisch	*French*
Grieche/Griechin	*Greek*
griechisch	*Greek*
Inder(in)	*Indian*
indisch	*Indian*
Ire/Irin	*Irish*
irisch	*Irish*

Had a look ☐ **Nearly there** ☐ **Nailed it** ☐

Italiener(in)	*Italian*
italienisch	*Italian*
Niederländer(in)	*Dutch*
niederländisch	*Dutch*
Österreicher(in)	*Austrian*
österreichisch	*Austrian*
Pakistani	*Pakistani*
pakistanisch	*Pakistani*
Russe/Russin	*Russian*
russisch	*Russian*
Schotte/Schottin	*Scottish*
schottisch	*Scottish*
Schweizer(in)	*Swiss*

High-frequency words

schweizerisch	*Swiss*	Betreff ...	*Regarding ...*
Spanier(in)	*Spanish*	In Bezug auf ...	*Further to / Following ...*
spanisch	*Spanish*	Zu Händen von ...	*For the attention of ...*
Türke/Türkin	*Turkish*		
türkisch	*Turkish*		
Waliser(in)	*Welsh*		
walisisch	*Welsh*		

Had a look ☐ **Nearly there** ☐ **Nailed it** ☐

das Telefon(e)	*telephone*
der Hörer(–)	*receiver (telephone)*
der Ton (Töne)	*tone*
die Vorwahl(en)	*area code*
die Telefonnummer wählen	*to dial the number*
im Gespräch mit	*in communication with*
am Apparat	*on the line / speaking*
der Augenblick(e)	*moment*
für jetzt	*for the moment*
falsche Nummer	*wrong number*
die SMS(–)	*text message*
simsen	*to text*
die E-Mail(s)	*email*
gesandt von	*sent by*
eigentlich	*in fact*

Places

Bayern	*Bavaria*
Köln	*Cologne*
München	*Munich*
Wien	*Vienna*
die Alpen	*the Alps*
der Schwarzwald	*the Black Forest*
die Donau	*the Danube*
der Rhein	*the Rhine*
der Bodensee	*Lake Constance*
der Ärmelkanal	*the English Channel*
der Eurotunnel	*the Channel Tunnel*

Had a look ☐ **Nearly there** ☐ **Nailed it** ☐

Social conventions

Guten Tag!	*Good day!*
Guten Abend!	*Good evening!*
Gute Nacht!	*Good night!*
Grüß Gott!	*Hello!*
Auf Wiedersehen!	*Goodbye!*
Bis später!	*See you later!*
Bis bald!	*See you soon!*
Bis morgen!	*See you tomorrow!*
Entschuldigung!	*Excuse me!*
Hilfe!	*Help!*
Wie bitte?	*I beg your pardon?*
Alles Gute!	*All the best!*
Mit bestem Gruß	*Best wishes*
bitte	*please*
danke schön	*thank you very much*
Bitte schön!	*You're welcome!*

Had a look ☐ **Nearly there** ☐ **Nailed it** ☐

Language used in dialogues and messages

Rufen Sie mich an!	*Call me! (formal)*
Ruf mich an!	*Call me! (informal)*
Kann ich etwas ausrichten?	*Can I take a message?*
Ich verbinde Sie.	*I will put you through.*
Ich höre zu.	*I'm listening.*
Ich bin gleich wieder da.	*I'll be right back.*
Warten Sie einen Moment.	*Wait a moment.*

Kapitel 1 Wörter

Words I should know for speaking and writing activities

Schulfächer	School subjects
Sprachen:	languages:
Deutsch	German
Englisch	English
Französisch	French
Spanisch	Spanish
Naturwissenschaft(en):	science(s):
Biologie	biology
Chemie	chemistry
Physik	physics
Mathe	maths
Mathe(matik)	math(ematic)s
Informatik	ICT
Geschichte	history
Erdkunde	geography
Kunst	art
Musik	music
Theater	drama
Religion	RE
Sport	PE, sport

Had a look ☐ Nearly there ☐ Nailed it ☐

Kleidung	Clothes
Ich trage (nie) …	I (never) wear…
einen Rock	a skirt
eine Jeans	jeans
eine Hose	trousers
eine Jacke	a jacket
eine Krawatte	a tie
ein Hemd	a shirt
ein Kleid	a dress
ein T-Shirt	a T-shirt
Sportschuhe	trainers
Schuhe	shoes

Had a look ☐ Nearly there ☐ Nailed it ☐

Das neue Schuljahr	The new school year
In der neunten Klasse freue ich mich (nicht) auf …	In Year 9, I'm (not) looking forward to …
den Matheunterricht	the maths lessons
die Klassenfahrt	the class trip
das Zeugnis	the report
die Hausaufgaben	the homework
die Klassenarbeiten	the tests
die Prüfungen	the exams
die Gruppen / die Clubs	the (after-school) groups / clubs
neue Fächer	new subjects
meine Freunde/ Freundinnen	my friends
total	totally
(echt) sehr	(really) very

(gar) nicht	not (at all)
nie	never
ein bisschen	a bit

Had a look ☐ Nearly there ☐ Nailed it ☐

weil er/sie/es … ist	because he/she/it is…
weil sie … sind	because they are …
langweilig	boring
stressig	stressful
schwierig	difficult
interessant	interesting
einfach	simple
prima	great
weil …	because …
es viele Klassenarbeiten gibt	there are lots of tests
wir in die Alpen fahren	we are going to the Alps
(Theater) mein Lieblingsfach ist	(drama) is my favourite subject
denn …	because …
sie sind mir wichtig	they are important to me
ich bekomme schlechte / gute Noten	I get bad / good grades
ich hatte letztes Jahr ein gutes / schlechtes Zeugnis	I had a good / bad report last year
das macht viel Spaß	it's a lot of fun

Had a look ☐ Nearly there ☐ Nailed it ☐

In den Sommerferien	In the summer holidays
Ich habe …	I …
(neue Bücher) gekauft	bought (new books)
(Gitarre) gelernt	learned (guitar)
(Fußball) gespielt	played (football)
nie (Hausaufgaben) gemacht	never did (homework)
immer (eine Mütze) getragen	always wore (a cap)
oft (einen Film) gesehen	often watched (a film)
Ich bin (in die Alpen) gefahren.	I went (to the Alps).
Ich hatte (ein Problem).	I had (a problem).
Das war (langweilig).	That was (boring).

Had a look ☐ Nearly there ☐ Nailed it ☐

Schulsachen	School items
Was hast du gekauft?	What have you bought?
Was hast du (für das neue Schuljahr) gekauft?	What have you bought (for the new school year)?
Ich habe … gekauft.	I bought …
einen Bleistift	a pencil
einen Kuli	a ballpoint pen

13

Kapitel 1 Wörter

einen Radiergummi — *a rubber*
einen Taschenrechner — *a calculator*
eine Schultasche — *a school bag*
ein Etui — *a pencil case*
Filzstifte — *felt-tip pens*

Had a look ☐   Nearly there ☐   Nailed it ☐

Ein Schultag / *A school day*

Was hat (die Klasse 9) in der (ersten) Stunde am (Montag)? — *What does (Year 9) have in the (first) lesson on (Monday)?*
Was hast du in der (zweiten) Stunde am (Dienstag)? — *What do you have in the (second) lesson on (Tuesday)?*
erste(n) — *first*
zweite(n) — *second*
dritte(n) — *third*
vierte(n) — *fourth*
fünfte(n) — *fifth*
sechste(n) — *sixth*
siebte(n) — *seventh*
Die Schule beginnt / endet um … — *School starts / ends at …*
nach der Pause — *after the break*
nach der Mittagspause — *after the lunch break*
Wir haben … Stunden pro Tag. — *We have … lessons per day.*
Jede Stunde dauert … Minuten. — *Each lesson lasts … minutes.*
Mein Lieblingsfach ist (Physik). — *My favourite subject is (physics).*
Ich bekomme immer gute Noten. — *I always get good grades.*
Ich mag (Chemie) (nicht). — *I (don't) like (chemistry).*
Ich mache (nicht) gern (Kunst). — *I (don't) like doing (art).*
Um wie viel Uhr? — *At what time?*
Hast du ein Lieblingsfach? — *Do you have a favourite subject?*
Welches Fach? — *Which subject?*

Had a look ☐   Nearly there ☐   Nailed it ☐

In der Schule / *At school*

der Computerraum — *ICT room*
der Schulhof — *playground*
die Aula — *assembly hall*
die Bibliothek — *library*
die Kantine — *canteen*
die Sporthalle — *sports hall*
das Klassenzimmer — *classroom*
das Labor — *lab(oratory)*
das Lehrerzimmer — *staff room*
die Toiletten — *toilets*

Had a look ☐   Nearly there ☐   Nailed it ☐

Die Schulordnung / *School rules*

Wir dürfen (nicht) … — *We are (not) allowed to …*
schlagen — *hit*
rauchen — *smoke*
essen — *eat*
trinken — *drink*
Wir dürfen keine Mützen tragen. — *We're not allowed to wear caps.*
Wir dürfen keinen Dialekt sprechen. — *We're not allowed to speak dialect.*
Wir müssen … — *We have to …*
pünktlich sein — *be punctual*
ruhig sein — *be quiet*
(un)gerecht — *(un)just*
(un)fair — *(un)fair*
Ich stimme da (nicht) zu. — *I (don't) agree.*
Du hast recht. — *You are right.*
Ich bin (nicht / ganz) deiner Meinung. — *I (don't / totally) agree with you.*
Nein, das finde ich …, weil … — *No, I find that … because …*
das (schrecklich) ist — *it's (terrible)*
ich das mag — *I like it*
denn … — *because …*
man muss (ruhig) sein — *you have to be (quiet)*
das ist (un)wichtig — *that's (un)important*

Had a look ☐   Nearly there ☐   Nailed it ☐

Eine Klassenfahrt / *A class trip*

Wir werden auf Austausch fahren. — *We will go on an exchange visit.*
Was werden wir am (Mittwoch) machen? — *What will we do on (Wednesday)?*
Ich werde … / Wir werden … — *I will … / We will …*
an einem Tag an der Schule lernen — *learn at school for a day*
den Abend bei einer Familie verbringen — *spend the evening with a family*
die Stadt besuchen — *visit the town*
in der Stadt bummeln — *stroll around the town*
eine Fahrradtour machen — *go on a cycling tour*
ins Hallenbad gehen — *go to the indoor swimming pool*
das Zirkusmuseum besuchen — *visit the circus museum*
die Sehenswürdigkeiten besichtigen — *visit the sights*
Andenken kaufen — *buy souvenirs*
(wieder) nach Hause fahren — *go home (again)*

Had a look ☐   Nearly there ☐   Nailed it ☐

14

Kapitel 1 Wörter

Erfolge feiern
Ich habe ...
Meine Schule / Klasse / Mannschaft hat ...
Die (Musik-)Gruppe hat ...
am (...-)Wettbewerb teilgenommen
in der Theatergruppe ein Theaterstück produziert
(ein erfolgreiches Konzert) gegeben
neue Mitglieder kennengelernt
die Prüfungen bestanden
den (ersten) Platz erreicht
Der Schulleiter / Die Lehrerin hat meine Eltern angerufen.
Ich bin ...
mit einer Medaille zurückgekommen
(in Englisch) durchgefallen
(letztes Jahr) sitzen geblieben
nicht sitzen geblieben
in (Mathe) nicht durchgefallen

Celebrating successes
I ...
My school / class / team ...
The (music) group ...
took part in the (...) competition
produced a play in the drama group
gave (a successful concert)
got to know new members
passed the exams
achieved (first) place, came (first)
The head teacher / teacher called my parents.
I ...
came back with a medal
failed (in English)
repeated the year (last year)
didn't repeat the year
didn't fail in (maths)

Had a look ☐ **Nearly there** ☐ **Nailed it** ☐

Totaler Erfolg im (Englisch-)Unterricht!
Die (Englisch-)Lehrerin/ Der (Englisch-)Lehrer war erstaunt!
Ich habe / Wir haben ...
Bonbons / Spiele als Resultat bekommen
im Restaurant gefeiert
Es gab eine Party.
Mein Foto war in der Zeitung.
In Zukunft werde ich ...
Nächstes Jahr werden wir ...
(an ...) teilnehmen
die Prüfungen bestehen

Complete success in (English)!
The (English) teacher was astonished!
I / We ...
received sweets / games as a result
celebrated in a restaurant
There was a party.
My photo was in the paper.
In the future I will ...
Next year we will ...
take part (in ...)
pass the exams

Had a look ☐ **Nearly there** ☐ **Nailed it** ☐

Das deutsche Schulsystem
die Grundschule
die Gesamtschule
die Hauptschule

die Realschule

das Gymnasium
die Oberstufe
das Abitur

The German school system
primary school
comprehensive school
a type of secondary modern school
a type of secondary modern school
grammar school
sixth form
German equivalent of A levels

Had a look ☐ **Nearly there** ☐ **Nailed it** ☐

K1

15

Kapitel 1 Wörter

Extra words I should know for reading and listening activities

Schulfächer und Schularbeit — *School subjects and school work*

die Fremdsprache(n) — *foreign language*
die Geisteswissenschaft(en) — *humanities (pl)*
Latein — *Latin*
die Medienwissenschaft — *media studies*
Technisches Zeichnen — *technical drawing*
das Turnen — *gymnastics*
Werken — *DT*
der Stundenplan — *timetable*
die Doppelstunde(n) — *double lesson*
das Arbeitsblatt(–blätter) — *worksheet*
das Experiment(e) — *experiment*
die Übung(en) — *exercise, practice*

Had a look ☐ Nearly there ☐ Nailed it ☐

Schulsachen — *School items*

der Anspitzer — *pencil sharpener*
das Heft(e) — *exercise book*
der Klebstoff — *glue*
der Kugelschreiber(–) — *biro, ballpoint pen*
die Schere(n) — *scissors*
der Schreibblock (–blöcke) — *paper pad*
die Schülerzeitung(en) — *school newspaper*

Had a look ☐ Nearly there ☐ Nailed it ☐

In der Schule — *At school*

anwesend — *present*
abwesend — *absent*
der/die Direktor(in) — *headteacher, principal*
der/die Schulleiter(in) — *headteacher, principal*
der Hausmeister(–) — *caretaker*
der/die Schüler(in) — *pupil*
die Schulferien (pl) — *school holidays*
das Semester(–) — *semester*
das Trimester(–) — *term*
der Gang (Gänge) — *corridor*
das Klassenzimmer(–) — *classroom*
das Sekretariat* — *(school) office, reception*
die Turnhalle — *gym*
der Umkleideraum (–räume) — *changing room*
die Versammlung(en) — *assembly*
der Projektor — *projector*
der Schreibtisch(e) — *desk*
der Stuhl (Stühle) — *chair*
die Tafel(n) — *(black / white) board*
der Tisch(e) — *table*

die Renovierung(en) — *renovation*
der Chor — *choir*
das Schulnetzwerk(e)** — *school network (Wi-Fi)*

Had a look ☐ Nearly there ☐ Nailed it ☐

Auf Austausch — *On an exchange*

der Austausch — *exchange*
der/die Austauschpartner(in) — *exchange partner*
der Ausweis — *identity card*
die Grenze(n) — *border*
der Reisepass — *passport*
die Radtour(en) — *cycling tour*
der Tagesausflug (–ausflüge) — *day trip*
der Basketballplatz (–plätze) — *basketball court*
das Freibad(–bäder) — *open-air swimming pool*
der Freizeitpark(s) — *amusement park*
der Sportplatz(–plätze) — *sports field, playing field*
der Tennisplatz(–plätze) — *tennis court*
der Internetanschluss (–anschlüsse) — *internet connection*
das WLAN — *Wi-Fi*
die Konsole(n) — *(games) console*
die Katastrophe(n) — *catastrophe*
reisekrank sein — *to be travel sick*
wandern — *to go hiking*

Had a look ☐ Nearly there ☐ Nailed it ☐

Schulleistungen — *School achievements*

die Durchschnittsnote(n) — *average grade*
befriedigend — *fair*
ausreichend — *satisfactory*
mangelhaft — *poor*
ungenügend — *unsatisfactory*
schwach — *weak, bad at (subject)*
stark — *strong, good at (subject)*
erfolgreich — *successful*
der Notendruck — *pressure to achieve good grades*
der Fortschritt(e) — *progress*
das Resultat(e) — *result*
nachsitzen — *to have detention*
das Abschlusszeugnis — *school leaving certificate*
die Mittlere Reife — *equivalent of GCSEs*
der Mittlere Schulabschluss — *equivalent of GCSEs*
der Schulabschluss — *school leaving certificate*

Had a look ☐ Nearly there ☐ Nailed it ☐

Kapitel 1 Wörter

Die Schulen | *Schools*

die Sekundarschule	*secondary school*
die staatliche Schule	*state school*
die Privatschule	*private school*
das Internat*	*boarding school*
der Kindergarten	*kindergarten, nursery school*
gemischt	*mixed*
die Ganztagsschule**	*school that lasts all day*

Had a look ☐ **Nearly there** ☐ **Nailed it** ☐

⭐ *Watch out for false friends! Sekretariat* might look like 'secretary', but it's actually the (school) office, or reception.

Similarly, *das Internat* looks very like 'internet', but means 'boarding school' in German.

⭐ **Break unfamiliar words down into their component parts to work out their meaning:

die Ganztagsschule → *ganz* (whole) + *Tag* (day) + *Schule* (school) = whole-day school (or, all-day school)

das Schulnetzwerk → *Schul(e)* (school) + *Netzwerk* (network) = *school* network

Kapitel 2 Wörter

Words I should know for speaking and writing activities

Freizeitaktivitäten	*Leisure activities*
Sport machen	to do sport
Sport treiben	to do sport
Fußball spielen	to play football
Hockey spielen	to play hockey
Basketball spielen	to play basketball
Schach spielen	to play chess
Karten spielen	to play cards
am Computer spielen	to play on the computer
auf dem Tablet spielen	to play on the tablet
auf dem Handy spielen	to play on the mobile phone
Computerspiele spielen	to play computer games
Freunde treffen	to meet friends
(Zeit) verbringen	to spend (time)
ins Kino gehen	to go to the cinema
in die Stadt gehen	to go into town
Musik machen	to make music
Musik hören	to listen to music
Bücher lesen	to read books
Zeitschriften lesen	to read magazines
fernsehen	to watch TV
Videos gucken	to watch videos
faulenzen	to laze around
nichts tun	to do nothing

Had a look ☐ **Nearly there** ☐ **Nailed it** ☐

Bücher	*Books*
die Biografie(n)	biography
der Comic(s)	comic book
der Fantasyroman(e)	fantasy novel
der Krimi(s)	detective / crime story
die Liebesgeschichte(n)	love story
das Magazin(e)	magazine
das Science-Fiction-Buch(–Bücher)	sci-fi book
die Zeitschrift(en)	magazine
die Zeitung(en)	newspaper

Had a look ☐ **Nearly there** ☐ **Nailed it** ☐

Instrumente	*Instruments*
die Blockflöte(n)	recorder
die Flöte(n)	flute
die Geige(n)	violin
die (elektrische) Gitarre(n)	(electric) guitar
die Klarinette(n)	clarinet
das Keyboard(s)	keyboard
das Klavier(e)	piano
das Saxofon(e)	saxophone
das Schlagzeug(e)	drums
die Trompete(n)	trumpet
Ich spiele kein Instrument.	I don't play an instrument.

Had a look ☐ **Nearly there** ☐ **Nailed it** ☐

Musik	*Music*
die Musikrichtung(en)	type of music
Ich höre (nicht) gern …	I (don't) like listening to …
Ich höre lieber …	I prefer to listen to …
Ich höre am liebsten …	I like listening to … best of all.
klassische Musik	classical music
Opernmusik	opera
Popmusik	pop music
Reggae	reggae
R&B	R&B
Rapmusik	rap
Heavy Metal	heavy metal
Country-und-Western-Musik	country and western
Jazzmusik	jazz
Livemusik	live music
Musik downloaden	to download music
die Musiksammlung(en)	music collection

Had a look ☐ **Nearly there** ☐ **Nailed it** ☐

Film und Fernsehen	*Film and television*
der Film(e)	film, movie
der Actionfilm(e)	action movie
der Fantasyfilm(e)	fantasy film
der Horrorfilm(e)	horror film
der Krimi(s)	detective / crime film
der Liebesfilm(e)	romance
der Science-Fiction-Film(e)	sci-fi film
der Thriller(–)	thriller
der Zeichentrickfilm(e)	cartoon
Ich sehe gern fern.	I like watching TV.
das Fernsehen	television
der Zuschauer(–)	viewer
die Fernsehsendung(en)	TV programme
die Dokumentation(en)	documentary
die Gameshow(s)	game show
die Komödie(n)	comedy
die Realityshow(s)	reality show
die Serie(n)	series
die Nachrichten (pl)	the news

Had a look ☐ **Nearly there** ☐ **Nailed it** ☐

Ich habe den Film … gefunden.	I found the film …
Ich habe die Sendung … gefunden.	I found the programme …
Der Film war …	The film was …
Die Sendung war …	The programme was …
Die Story war …	The story / plot was …
Die Schauspieler waren …	The actors were …

Kapitel 2 Wörter

Die Charaktere waren …	The characters were …
furchtbar	terrible
großartig	great
langweilig	boring
schwach	weak
(un)realistisch	(un)realistic
Ich empfehle den Film / die Sendung, weil …	I recommend the film / programme because …

Had a look ☐ Nearly there ☐ Nailed it ☐

Sport / Sport

Ski fahren	to go skiing
snowboarden	to go snowboarding
eislaufen	to ice skate
wandern	to hike
klettern	to climb
schwimmen	to swim
Fahrrad / Rad fahren	to cycle
Handball spielen	to play handball
Tennis spielen	to play tennis
Ich möchte …	I would like …
in den Bergen wandern	to go hiking in the mountains
an den Felsen klettern	to go rock climbing
Ich spiele gern (Fußball).	I like playing (football).
Ich (fahre) gern (Ski).	I like (skiing).
Ich (fahre) nicht gern (Rad).	I (don't) like (cycling).
Ich turne (sehr) gern.	I (very much) like doing gymnastics.
Ich spiele seit (fünf Jahren) (Tennis).	I have been playing (tennis) (for five years).
Ich trainiere (jeden Tag) im Verein.	I train at the club (every day).
Ich trainiere (einmal pro Woche) in einer Mannschaft.	I train in a team (once a week).
Ich möchte bestimmt (Skateboard fahren).	I would definitely like to (go skateboarding).
Ich möchte nie (snowboarden).	I would never like to (go snowboarding).
Ich habe (diese Woche) (Eislaufen) ausprobiert.	I tried (ice skating) (this week).
Ich habe (gestern) (Klettern) ausprobiert.	I tried (climbing) (yesterday).

Had a look ☐ Nearly there ☐ Nailed it ☐

Feste und Feiertage / Celebrations and holidays

am 24. Dezember (usw.)	on the 24th December (etc.)
feiern	to celebrate
Silvester	New Year's Eve
zu Ostern	at Easter
zu Weihnachten	at Christmas
der Feiertag(e)	public holiday
das Fest(e)	festival, fair
der Festzug(–züge)	procession
die Fete(n)	party
die Feier(n)	celebration
das Feuerwerk(e)	fireworks (pl)
das Geschenk(e)	present
der Karneval	carnival
die Kerze(n)	candle
die Spezialität(en)	speciality
das Spielzeug(e) (aus Holz)	(wooden) toy
die Stimmung(en)	atmosphere
die Tradition(en)	tradition
das Volksfest(e)	(traditional) fair
der Weihnachtsmarkt (–märkte)	Christmas market
der Weihnachtsschmuck	Christmas decorations

Had a look ☐ Nearly there ☐ Nailed it ☐

Extra words I should know for reading and listening activities

Freizeitaktivitäten — Leisure activities
- sich amüsieren — to have fun
- (sich) entspannen — to relax
- Interesse haben an — to be interested in
- im Internet chatten — to chat online
- im Internet surfen — to surf online
- das Eintrittsgeld — entry fee
- die Eintrittskarte(n) — entry ticket
- der Jugendklub(s) — youth club
- die Unterhaltung — entertainment

Had a look ☐ Nearly there ☐ Nailed it ☐

Musik hören — Listening to music
- die Festplatte(n) — hard drive
- die Kopfhörer (pl) — headphones
- der Lautsprecher(–) — (loud)speaker
- das Lied(er) — song
- der Ton — sound
- die Volksmusik — folk music
- die neunziger Jahre — the nineties
- Platz sparen — to save space
- üben — to practise

Had a look ☐ Nearly there ☐ Nailed it ☐

Film und Fernsehen — Film and TV
- der Abenteuerfilm(e) — adventure film
- der Bildschirm(e) — screen (TV, computer)
- der Fernseher(–) — television (set)
- die Kurzfassung(en) — summary
- die Leinwand(–wände) — (big) screen (in cinema)
- die Originalfassung(en) — original version
- der Sitz(platz) — seat (in cinema, etc.)
- mit Untertiteln — with subtitles
- beeindruckend — impressive
- begabt — talented
- gruselig — creepy, scary
- lebhaft — lively
- unterhaltsam — entertaining
- witzig — witty

Had a look ☐ Nearly there ☐ Nailed it ☐

Sport — Sport
- angeln — to fish
- fechten — to fence
- kegeln — (nine-pin) bowling
- rennen — to run
- ringen — to wrestle
- rodeln — to go tobogganing
- Rollschuh laufen — to go roller skating
- rudern — to row
- schießen — to shoot
- segeln — to sail
- tauchen — to dive
- turnen — to do gymnastics
- der Federball — badminton
- der Korbball — netball
- die Sportart(en) — type of sport

Had a look ☐ Nearly there ☐ Nailed it ☐

Feste und Feiertage — Celebrations and holidays
- der Neujahrstag — New Year's Day
- der Karfreitag — Good Friday
- der Ostersonntag — Easter Sunday
- der Maifeiertag — May Day
- der Muttertag — Mother's Day
- der Tag der Deutschen Einheit — Day of German Unity
- der Nikolaustag — St Nicholas' Day (6th December)
- das Osterei(er) — Easter egg
- der Osterhase — Easter bunny
- die Wiedervereinigung* — reunification
- die Einladung(en) — invitation
- die Rede(n) — speech
- der Umzug(–züge) — street procession
- einladen — to invite
- schmücken — to decorate
- sich verkleiden — to dress up

Had a look ☐ Nearly there ☐ Nailed it ☐

Auf dem Weihnachtsmarkt — At the Christmas market
- der Adventskranz — advent wreath
- der Weihnachtsbaum(–bäume) — Christmas tree
- das Weihnachtslied(er) — Christmas carol
- die Wollmütze(n) — woolly hat
- der Imbiss(e) — snack
- die Bratwurst(–würste) — fried sausage
- der Glühwein — mulled wine
- der Kinderpunsch — non-alcoholic punch
- der Lebkuchen — gingerbread
- die Waffel(n) — waffle
- kandierte Äpfel — candied apples
- geröstete Mandeln — roasted almonds

Had a look ☐ Nearly there ☐ Nailed it ☐

> ⭐ *Don't be daunted by long, tricky-looking words. Look carefully at the words they are made up of and try to work out the meaning based on the words you know.
>
> *die Wiedervereinigung*
> You know that *wieder* means 'again' and *der Verein* is 'club' (i.e. somewhere where people come together), so *Wiedervereinigung* is literally 'the coming together again', or 'reunification'.
> *Am 3. Oktober feiert man die Wiedervereinigung Deutschlands.* On 3rd October, we celebrate the reunification of Germany.

Kapitel 3 Wörter

Words I should know for speaking and writing activities

Charaktereigen-schaften	***Personal characteristics***
Er/Sie ist (nicht) …	*He/She is (not)…*
aktiv	*active*
cool	*cool*
dynamisch	*dynamic*
fleißig	*hard-working*
frech	*cheeky*
freundlich	*friendly*
intelligent	*intelligent*
kreativ	*creative*
langweilig	*boring*
lustig	*funny*
nett	*nice*
originell	*original*
sportlich	*sporty*
toll	*great*
ziemlich	*quite*
sehr	*very*
nie	*never*
relativ	*relatively*
total	*totally*

Had a look ☐ Nearly there ☐ Nailed it ☐

Aussehen	***Appearance***
Er/Sie hat … Haare.	*He/She has … hair.*
blonde	*blonde*
braune	*brown*
schwarze	*black*
rote	*red*
lange	*long*
kurze	*short*
Er/Sie hat … Augen.	*He/She has … eyes.*
graue	*grey*
blaue	*blue*
grüne	*green*
Er/Sie trägt …	*He/She wears …*
eine (modische) Brille	*(trendy) glasses*
eine (coole) Sonnenbrille	*(cool) sunglasses*
Er hat einen (großen) Bart.	*He has a (big) beard.*
Er/Sie ist …	*He/She is …*
schlank	*slim*
groß	*big, tall*
klein	*small, short*

Had a look ☐ Nearly there ☐ Nailed it ☐

Wie ist ein guter Freund/eine gute Freundin?	***What makes a good friend?***
Ein guter Freund/Eine gute Freundin …	*A good friend …*
muss Zeit für mich haben	*must have time for me*
muss sympathisch sein	*must be nice*
muss mich immer unterstützen	*must always support me*
muss viel Geduld haben	*must have lots of patience*
muss die gleichen Interessen haben	*must have the same interests*
kann mit mir über alles reden	*can talk to me about anything*
darf nicht eifersüchtig sein	*isn't allowed to be jealous*
Das ist für mich …	*That is … to me.*
nicht wichtig	*not important*
wichtig	*important*
sehr wichtig	*very important*
die Kommunikation	*communication*

Had a look ☐ Nearly there ☐ Nailed it ☐

Beziehungen	***Relationships***
Ich verstehe mich gut mit …	*I get on well with …*
Ich verstehe mich nicht so gut mit …	*I don't get on so well with …*
meiner Mutter	*my mother*
meinem Vater	*my father*
meiner Stiefmutter	*my stepmother*
meinem Stiefvater	*my stepfather*
meinen Eltern	*my parents*
meiner Schwester	*my sister*
meinem Bruder	*my brother*
meiner Halbschwester	*my half-sister*
meinem Halbbruder	*my half-brother*
meinen Geschwistern	*my siblings*
meiner Großmutter	*my grandmother*
meinem Großvater	*my grandfather*
meiner Oma	*my grandma*
meinem Opa	*my grandpa*
meinen Großeltern	*my grandparents*
meiner Tante	*my aunt*
meinem Onkel	*my uncle*
meinen Cousins/Cousinen	*my cousins*

Had a look ☐ Nearly there ☐ Nailed it ☐

… weil er/sie … ist.	*… because he/she is …*
dynamisch	*dynamic*
eifersüchtig	*jealous*
langweilig	*boring*
launisch	*moody*
nervig	*annoying*
streng	*strict*
sympathisch	*kind, nice*
… weil er/sie …	*… because he/she …*
(viel / keine) Geduld hat	*has (a lot of / no) patience*

K 3

Kapitel 3 Wörter

(immer / nie) Zeit für mich hat	(always / never) has time for me	Er/Sie hat vielen Leuten geholfen.	He/She helped lots of people.
mich unterstützt	supports me	Er/Sie ist ...	He/She is ...
mich nicht unterstützt	doesn't support me	begabt	gifted, talented
mir auf die Nerven geht	gets on my nerves	berühmt	famous

Had a look ☐ Nearly there ☐ Nailed it ☐

		diszipliniert	disciplined
		erfolgreich	successful
		sehr fit	very fit
Wir/Sie haben eine tolle Beziehung.	We/They have a great relationship.	eine Inspiration	an inspiration
		intelligent	intelligent
Ich streite mich mit (ihr).	I argue with (her).	Ich finde das oberflächlich.	I find that superficial.
Er/Sie streitet sich mit (ihm).	He/She argues with (him).	Meiner Meinung nach ...	In my opinion, ...
Sie streiten sich mit (ihnen).	They argue with (them).	sind Sportler sehr gute Vorbilder	sportspeople are very good role models
Ich werde mich mit (...) besser verstehen.	I will get on better with (...).	sind Models keine guten Vorbilder	models are not good role models
Er/Sie sagt, ...	He/She says ...	haben Vorbilder einen positiven / negativen Einfluss	role models have a positive / negative influence
Sie sagen, ...	They say ...		
ich mache nicht genug Hausaufgaben	I don't do enough homework	Vorbilder sind für mich wichtig, weil ...	Role models are important to me because ...
ich verbringe zu viel Zeit (mit dem Handy / vor dem Fernseher)	I spend too much time (on my mobile phone / in front of the TV)	sie eine Inspiration sind	they are an inspiration
		sie vielen Leuten helfen	they help lots of people
ich darf (den Computer / mein Handy) nicht benutzen	I'm not allowed to use (the computer / my mobile phone)	Vorbilder sind für mich nicht wichtig, weil ...	Role models are not important to me because ...
ich darf nicht (Fußball spielen / ausgehen)	I'm not allowed to (play football / go out)	sie oberflächlich sind	they are superficial
		sie in der Realität nicht existieren	they don't exist in reality

Had a look ☐ Nearly there ☐ Nailed it ☐

Had a look ☐ Nearly there ☐ Nailed it ☐

Vorbilder / Role models

Er/Sie ist mein großes Vorbild.	He/She is my great role model.
Er/Sie inspiriert mich.	He/She inspires me.
Sie inspirieren mich sehr.	They inspire me greatly.
Ich bewundere ihn/sie sehr.	I admire him/her a lot.
Ich mag ihn/sie.	I like him/her.
Ich finde ihn/sie beeindruckend, weil ...	I find him/her impressive because ...
er/sie ein toller Sportler / eine tolle Sportlerin ist	he/she is a great sportsperson
er/sie intelligent ist	he/she is intelligent
er/sie fleißig ist	he/she is hard-working
er/sie mich unterstützt	he/she supports me
er/sie sich für ... interessiert	he/she is interested in ...
er/sie vielen Leuten hilft	he/she helps lots of people
die Schule für ihn/sie sehr wichtig war	school was very important for him/her
er/sie immer gegen Gewalt war	he/she was always against violence

Dein Leben jetzt und als Kind / Your life now and as a child

Als ich vier Jahre alt war, konnte ich ...	When I was four years old, I could...
Rad fahren	ride a bike
(nicht) sehr gut schwimmen	(not) swim very well
(schon) Spanisch sprechen	(already) speak Spanish
Als ich ein Kind war, musste ich ...	When I was a child, I had to ...
immer zu Hause helfen	always help at home
um 20:00 Uhr zu Hause sein	be home by 8 p.m.
jeden Abend meine Hausaufgaben machen	do my homework every evening
früher ins Bett gehen	go to bed earlier
Als ich ein Kind war, musste ich keine Hausaufgaben machen.	When I was a child, I didn't have to do homework.
Als ich jünger war, durfte ich ...	When I was younger, I was allowed to ...

Had a look ☐ Nearly there ☐ Nailed it ☐

Kapitel 3 Wörter

fernsehen	*watch TV*
am Computer spielen	*play on the computer*
allein in die Schule gehen	*go to school on my own*
Als ich jünger war, durfte ich …	*When I was younger, I was not allowed to …*
keine Zeit mit meinen Freunden verbringen	*spend time with my friends*
am Wochenende nicht mit meinen Freunden in die Stadt gehen	*go into town at the weekend with my friends*
nicht zu spät nach Hause kommen	*come home too late*
am Abend nicht mit Freunden ins Kino gehen	*go to the cinema with friends in the evening*

Had a look ☐ **Nearly there** ☐ **Nailed it** ☐

Jetzt kann ich …	*Now I can …*
Am Wochenende darf ich (nicht) …	*At the weekend I am (not) allowed to …*
Am Abend muss ich …	*In the evening I must …*
früh ins Bett gehen	*go to bed early*
spät ins Bett gehen	*go to bed late*
viele Hausaufgaben machen	*do lots of homework*
ins Kino gehen	*go to the cinema*
einkaufen gehen	*go shopping*
in den Park gehen	*go to the park*
Zeit mit Freunden verbringen	*spend time with friends*
(sehr gut) Fußball spielen	*play football (very well)*
viel trainieren	*train a lot*
online chatten	*chat online*
online surfen	*surf online*
Am Abend muss ich …	*In the evening I don't have to …*
keine Hausaufgaben machen	*do homework*
Das finde ich …	*I find that …*
viel besser	*much better*
fair	*fair*
unfair	*unfair*

Had a look ☐ **Nearly there** ☐ **Nailed it** ☐

Extra words I should know for reading and listening activities

Positive Charakter-eigenschaften	*Positive personal characteristics*
abenteuerlich	adventurous
ehrlich	honest
gesprächig	chatty
hilfsbereit	helpful
höflich	polite
humorvoll*	humorous, witty
klug	clever
lebendig	lively
lieb	kind
optimistisch*	optimistic
selbstständig	independent
unternehmungslustig	adventurous, likes doing lots of things
vernünftig	reasonable
guter Laune sein	to be in a good mood

Had a look ☐   Nearly there ☐   Nailed it ☐

Negative Charakter-eigenschaften	*Negative personal characteristics*
böse	nasty, bad
egoistisch*	selfish
ernst	serious
gemein*	mean
humorlos*	humourless, without a sense of humour
pessimistisch*	pessimistic
rechthaberisch	bossy
schüchtern	shy
schwatzhaft	gossipy, chatty
selbstsüchtig	selfish
still	quiet
unartig	naughty
schlechter Laune sein	to be in a bad mood

Had a look ☐   Nearly there ☐   Nailed it ☐

Aussehen	*Appearance*
altmodisch	old-fashioned
dünn	thin
flott	jaunty, smart
gepflegt	smart, neat, well-groomed
glatt	straight, smooth
hässlich	ugly
hübsch	pretty
lockig	curly
schick	smart, chic, trendy
unordentlich	messy
eine Glatze haben	to be bald
ein Piercing haben	to have a piercing
das Gesicht(er)	face

der Ohrring(e)	earring
der Oberlippenbart	moustache
der Schnurrbart	moustache

Had a look ☐   Nearly there ☐   Nailed it ☐

Freundschaften und Beziehungen	*Friendships and relationships*
der/die feste Freund(in)	boyfriend/girlfriend
der Freundeskreise(e)	circle of friends
das Geheimnis(–nisse)	secret
der Kerl	guy, dude, bloke
der/die Prominente(n)*	celebrity, VIP
der Typ	guy, dude, bloke
die Unterstützung	support
das Verhältnis(–nisse)	relationship
bekannt	well-known
berühmt	famous
sich ärgern	to be annoyed
auskommen mit	to get on with
sich entschuldigen	to apologise
erlauben	to allow
sich fühlen**	to feel
sich kümmern um	to look after
Respekt haben (vor)	to respect
sorgen für	to care for, to look after
vergeben	to forgive
Ich kann ... nicht leiden.	I can't stand ...

Had a look ☐   Nearly there ☐   Nailed it ☐

Familienmitglieder	*Family members*
der/die Erwachsene	adult
der Ehemann	husband
der Mann	man, husband
die Ehefrau	wife
die Frau	woman, wife
der/die Jugendliche	youth, young person
das Kind(er)	child
das Einzelkind(er)	only child
das Enkelkind(er)	grandchild
das Baby(s)	baby
der Sohn (Söhne)	son
die Tochter (Töchter)	daughter
der Schwiegersohn	son-in-law
die Schwiegertochter	daughter-in-law
der Schwager	brother-in-law
die Schwägerin	sister-in-law
der Neffe(n)	nephew
die Nichte(n)	niece
der Zwilling(e)	twin

Had a look ☐   Nearly there ☐   Nailed it ☐

Kapitel 3 Wörter

Familienstand	*Marital status*
single	*single*
ledig	*unmarried*
unverheiratet	*unmarried*
verliebt	*in love*
verlobt	*engaged*
verheiratet	*married*
getrennt	*separated*
geschieden	*divorced*
sich verloben	*to get engaged*
heiraten	*to get married*
sich trennen	*to separate, to split up*
sich scheiden lassen	*to get divorced*

Had a look ☐ Nearly there ☐ Nailed it ☐

K 3

*Look for cognates and near-cognates when working out meanings of new words.

Humorvoll looks similar to the two English words 'humour' and 'full', and means 'humorous'. And *humorlos* means 'humorless'.

Optimistisch and *pessimistisch* should be easy to work out. And can you see the link between *gemein* and 'mean', or *egoistisch* and 'selfish' (or 'egotistical')?

Have a look at *der/die Prominente*. This is a near-cognate, literally meaning 'prominent person', or 'celebrity/VIP'.

**Don't mistake *sich fühlen* for *fühlen*. Both translate as 'to feel', but *sich fühlen* relates to how you feel (yourself), *fühlen* relates to what you feel or sense.

*Ich **fühle mich** gut.* I feel fine.

*Ich **fühle** einen Schmerz.* I feel a pain.

Kapitel 4 Wörter

Words I should know for speaking and writing activities

Zu Hause | At home
das Arbeitszimmer — *study*
das Badezimmer — *bathroom*
der Dachboden — *attic / loft*
die Dusche — *shower*
das Esszimmer — *dining room*
die Garage — *garage*
der Garten — *garden*
die Küche — *kitchen*
das Schlafzimmer — *bedroom*
das Wohnzimmer — *sitting room*
der Flur — *hall / corridor*

Had a look ☐ **Nearly there** ☐ **Nailed it** ☐

Ich wohne (seit vier Jahren) … — *I have been living … (for four years).*
in einer Kleinstadt — *in a small town*
in einer Großstadt — *in a city*
in der Stadtmitte — *in the town centre*
am Stadtrand — *on the outskirts of town / in the suburbs*
auf dem Land — *in the countryside*
in einem Einfamilienhaus — *in a detached house*
in einer Doppelhaushälfte — *in a semi-detached house*
in einem Reihenhaus — *in a terraced house*
in einem Hochhaus — *in a high-rise building*
in einem Wohnblock — *in a block of flats*
Im Erdgeschoss gibt es … — *On the ground floor there is …*
Im ersten Stock gibt es … — *On the first floor there is …*
Wir haben keinen Tennisplatz. — *We don't have a tennis court.*

Had a look ☐ **Nearly there** ☐ **Nailed it** ☐

Auf Austausch | On an exchange visit
Herzlich willkommen in (Deutschland)! — *Welcome to (Germany)!*
Wie geht's dir / Ihnen? — *How are you?*
Wie bitte? — *Pardon?*
Ich verstehe deine / Ihre Frage nicht. — *I don't understand your question.*
Hast du / Haben Sie Hunger? — *Are you hungry?*
Hast du / Haben Sie Durst? — *Are you thirsty?*
Kannst du / Können Sie bitte langsamer sprechen? — *Can you speak more slowly, please?*
Kannst du / Können Sie das bitte wiederholen? — *Can you repeat that, please?*
Was bedeutet ‚Hausschuhe'? — *What does 'Hausschuhe' mean?*
Wie heißt ‚Wi-Fi-Code' auf Deutsch? — *How do you say 'WiFi code' in German?*

Had a look ☐ **Nearly there** ☐ **Nailed it** ☐

Man muss in der Ruhezeit ruhig sein. — *We must be quiet during 'quiet time'.*
die Hausordnung — *house rules*
die Mittagsruhe — *quiet time at midday*
die Ruhezeit — *quiet time*
Man darf im Schlafzimmer keine laute Musik spielen. — *We are not allowed to play loud music in the bedroom.*
Man darf kein Instrument üben. — *We are not allowed to practise an instrument.*
Man darf nicht mit dem Ball spielen. — *We are not allowed to play ball games.*
Man darf nie das Auto vor der Garage waschen. — *We are never allowed to wash the car in front of the garage.*
Am Feiertag / Den ganzen Tag ist Ruhezeit! — *On a bank holiday / The whole day it is quiet time!*

Had a look ☐ **Nearly there** ☐ **Nailed it** ☐

Der Tagesablauf | Daily routine
an einem Schultag — *on a school day*
am Wochenende — *at the weekend*
täglich — *daily*
am Abend / Nachmittag — *in the evening / afternoon*
nach der Schule / dem Abendessen — *after school / dinner*
aufstehen — *to get up*
frühstücken — *to have breakfast*
abfahren — *to leave*
fernsehen — *to watch TV*
sich setzen — *to sit down, take a seat*
sich an den Computer setzen — *to sit down at the computer*
am Computer sitzen — *to sit at the computer*
sich amüsieren — *to have a good time*
sich langweilen — *to be bored*
sich mit Freunden treffen — *to meet up with friends*
… Stunden in der Schule verbringen — *to spend … hours at school*

Had a look ☐ **Nearly there** ☐ **Nailed it** ☐

Kapitel 4 Wörter

Essen und trinken	*Eating and drinking*
Das Frühstück / Mittagessen / Abendessen / Abendbrot essen wir um …	*We eat breakfast / lunch / dinner at …*
Ich esse / Wir essen …	*I / We eat …*
auf der Terrasse	*on the terrace / patio*
bei uns im Esszimmer	*at home in the dining room*
auf dem Weg zur Schule	*on the way to school*
vor dem Fernseher	*in front of the TV*
Das hat … geschmeckt.	*It tasted …*
ekelhaft / schrecklich	*disgusting / dreadful*
köstlich / wunderbar / lecker	*delicious / wonderful / tasty*
salzig / süß / würzig	*salty / sweet / spicy*
auswählen	*to choose*
einkaufen	*to buy, to shop*
vorbereiten	*to prepare*

Had a look ☐ **Nearly there** ☐ **Nailed it** ☐

das Brot	*bread*
der Käse	*cheese*
die Kartoffelchips (pl)	*crisps*
die Suppe	*soup*
die Hauptspeise	*main course*
der Braten	*roast (meat)*
die Currywurst	*sausage with curry sauce*
der Fisch	*fish*
das Schnitzel	*schnitzel / escalope*
ein gemischter Salat	*mixed salad*
das Spiegelei(er)	*fried egg*
die Wurst	*sausage*
(mit) Kartoffeln / Reis / Pommes	*(with) potatoes / rice / chips*
die Nachspeise	*dessert*
das Eis	*ice cream*
das Gebäck	*baked goods / pastries*
der Keks(e)	*biscuit*
die Torte(n)	*gâteau / flan*
der Zucchinikuchen	*courgette cake*
der Pampelmusensaft	*grapefruit juice*
der Tee	*tea*
die (Voll-)Milch	*(full-fat) milk*

Had a look ☐ **Nearly there** ☐ **Nailed it** ☐

Obst und Gemüse	*Fruit and vegetables*
das Obst	*fruit*
das Gemüse	*vegetables*
die Gurke(n)	*cucumber*
die Karotte(n)	*carrot*
der Kohl(e)	*cabbage*
die Paprika(s)	*pepper*
die Tomate(n)	*tomato*
die Zwiebel(n)	*onion*
der Apfel (Äpfel)	*apple*
die Banane(n)	*banana*
die Birne(n)	*pear*
die Erdbeere(n)	*strawberry*
die Orange(n)	*orange*
der Pfirsich(e)	*peach*

Had a look ☐ **Nearly there** ☐ **Nailed it** ☐

Soziale Netzwerke und Technologie	*Social media and technology*
Wie kommunizierst du am liebsten?	*How do you most like to communicate?*
Ich nutze soziale Netzwerke.	*I use social networks.*
Ich simse (meinen Eltern).	*I text (my parents).*
Ich sende E-Mails.	*I send emails.*
Ich telefoniere per Internet.	*I call via the internet.*
Ich rufe (meine Freunde) vom Handy an.	*I call (my friends) on my mobile.*
Ich habe persönliche Gespräche.	*I have face-to-face conversations.*
…, wenn …	*… if …*
ich mich langweile	*I'm bored*
ich mit meinen Freunden rede / spreche	*I talk to my friends*
ich spät bin	*I'm late*
ich unterwegs bin	*I'm on the way / out and about*

Had a look ☐ **Nearly there** ☐ **Nailed it** ☐

Das ist …	*That is …*
nützlich	*useful*
lustig	*funny*
unterhaltsam	*entertaining*
wichtig	*important*
praktisch	*practical*
Das macht Spaß.	*That's fun.*
online / im Internet chatten	*to chat online*
im Internet surfen	*to surf online*
Fotos hochladen	*to upload photos*
Musik herunterladen	*to download music*
der Bildschirm	*screen*
der Desktop-PC	*desktop computer, PC*
die Digitalkamera	*digital camera*
das Handy	*mobile phone*
der MP3-Player	*MP3 player*
der Streaming-Dienst	*streaming service*
das Smart-TV	*smart TV*
das Tablet	*tablet*
die Konsole	*console*

Had a look ☐ **Nearly there** ☐ **Nailed it** ☐

Kapitel 4 Wörter

Vor- und Nachteile der Technologie
Advantages and disadvantages of technology

Ich finde es positiv / negativ, dass …	*I find it positive / negative that …*
Ein großer Vorteil der Technologie ist, dass …	*A big advantage of technology is that …*
Ein großer Nachteil ist, dass …	*A big disadvantage is that …*
Es gibt Vorteile und Nachteile.	*There are advantages and disadvantages.*
einerseits	*on the one hand*
auf der anderen Seite	*on the other hand*
Man langweilt sich nie.	*You never get bored.*
Man amüsiert sich sehr gut am Bildschirm.	*You entertain yourself very well on screen.*
Technologie ist extrem teuer.	*Technology is extremely expensive.*
Man bleibt mit Leuten in Kontakt.	*You stay in contact with people.*
Man ist nicht so oft draußen aktiv.	*You're not active outside so often.*
Man findet Informationen schnell online.	*You find information quickly online.*
Das Internet führt manchmal zu Internet-Mobbing.	*The internet sometimes leads to cyberbullying.*
Das persönliche Leben bleibt nie privat.	*Your personal life never stays private.*

Had a look ☐ **Nearly there** ☐ **Nailed it** ☐

Extra words I should know for reading and listening activities

Zu Hause	**At home**
der Eingang(-gänge)	entrance
der Rasen(-)	lawn
der Wintergarten	conservatory
die Treppe*	(flight of) stairs, staircase
die Etage(n)	floor, storey
die Decke(n)	ceiling
der Fußboden	floor (ground)
die Heizung	heating
die Mauer(n)	wall (outside)
die Tür(en)	door
die Wand (Wände)	wall (inside)
aufräumen	to tidy up
mähen	to mow (lawn)
sauber machen	to clean
möbliert	furnished
renoviert	renovated

Had a look ☐ Nearly there ☐ Nailed it ☐

Möbel*	**Furniture**
das Mobiliar*	furnishings (pl)
das Etagenbett	bunk bed
die Kommode(n)	chest of drawers
der Nachttisch(e)	bedside table
das Regal(e)	shelf
die Schuhblade(n)	drawer
der Schuhschrank (-schränke)	shoe cupboard
die Badewanne(n)	bathtub
das Waschbecken(-)	washbasin
der Backofen(-öfen)	oven
der Herd(e)	cooker
das Kochfeld(er)	hob
der Kühlschrank (-schränke)	fridge
die Mikrowelle(n)	microwave oven
die Waschmaschine(n)	washing machine
der Spiegel(-)	mirror
der Teppich(e)	carpet
der Vorhang (Vorhänge)	curtain

Had a look ☐ Nearly there ☐ Nailed it ☐

Soziale Netzwerke und Technologie	**Social media and technology**
der Anrufbeantworter(-)	(telephone) answering machine
der Drucker(-)	printer
der Klingelton(e)	ringtone
die Medien (pl)	media
das Netz	net
das Postfach(-fächer)	mail box (email)
das Smartphone(s)	smartphone
die Smartuhr(en)	smart watch
die Startseite	homepage (internet)
der Telefonanruf (-anrufe)	telephone call
anrufen	to call, to ring
(aus)drucken	to print (out)
eingeben	to enter (data into computer/phone)
empfangen	to receive
löschen	to delete
speichern	to save (data on computer)

Had a look ☐ Nearly there ☐ Nailed it ☐

Vor- und Nachteile der Technologie	**Advantages and disadvantages of technology**
die Daten (pl)	data
die Entwicklung(en)	development
die Gefahr(en)	danger
der Missbrauch (-bräuche)	abuse
das Risiko(s)	risk
der Schutz	protection
die Schwiergkeit(en)	difficulty
entwickeln	to develop
funktionieren	to work
missbrauchen	to abuse
teilen	to share
lehrreich	informative, instructive, educational
verboten	forbidden

Had a look ☐ Nearly there ☐ Nailed it ☐

> *Look out for nouns which are singular in German but plural in English, and vice versa:
>
> die Treppe (singular) → (flight of) stairs
>
> das Möbilar (singular) → furnishings
>
> die Möbel (plural) → furniture

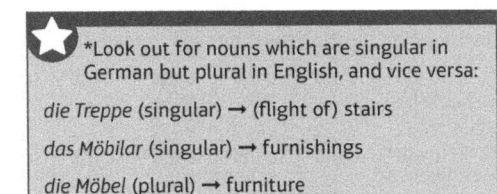

Kapitel 5 Wörter

Words I should know for speaking and writing activities

Verkehrsmittel — *Forms of transport*
Ich fahre ... — *I travel ...*
mit dem Zug / Bus / Auto / Rad — *by train / bus / car / bike*
mit der U-Bahn / S-Bahn / Straßenbahn — *by underground / urban railway / tram*
Ich fliege mit dem Flugzeug. — *I fly.*
Ich gehe zu Fuß. — *I go on foot. / I walk.*

Had a look ☐ Nearly there ☐ Nailed it ☐

Hotelzimmer reservieren — *Booking hotel rooms*
Ich möchte ... reservieren. — *I would like to reserve ...*
ein Einzelzimmer — *a single room*
zwei Doppelzimmer — *two double rooms*
für eine Nacht — *for one night*
für zwei Nächte vom 8. bis 10. Januar — *for two nights from 8 to 10 January*
Möchten Sie ... reservieren? — *Would you like to reserve ...?*
einen Parkplatz — *a parking space*
ein Zimmer mit Aussicht — *a room with a view*
Gibt es WLAN / ein Restaurant im Hotel? — *Is there Wi-Fi / a restaurant in the hotel?*
Wann ist das Restaurant geöffnet? — *When is the restaurant open?*
Um wie viel Uhr gibt es Frühstück? — *What time is breakfast?*

Had a look ☐ Nearly there ☐ Nailed it ☐

Komparative — *Comparatives*
bequemer — *more comfortable*
besser — *better*
billiger — *cheaper*
größer — *bigger*
länger — *longer*
langsamer — *slower*
näher — *nearer*
praktischer — *more practical*
schneller — *quicker*
teurer — *more expensive*
umweltfreundlicher — *more environmentally friendly*
lieber — *prefer*

Had a look ☐ Nearly there ☐ Nailed it ☐

Superlative — *Superlatives*
am besten — *best*
am bequemsten — *most comfortable*
am billigsten — *cheapest*
am einfachsten — *easiest*
am größten — *biggest*
am längsten — *longest*
am nächsten — *nearest*
am schnellsten — *quickest*
am teuersten — *most expensive*
am umweltfreundlichsten — *most environmentally friendly*
am wichtigsten — *most important*
am liebsten — *like the most*

Had a look ☐ Nearly there ☐ Nailed it ☐

Fahrkarten kaufen — *Buying train tickets*
Ich möchte eine Fahrkarte nach Berlin, bitte. — *I'd like a ticket to Berlin, please.*
Einfach oder hin und zurück? — *Single or return?*
Wann fährt der nächste Zug ab? — *When does the next train leave?*
Der Zug fährt um 12:51 Uhr ab. — *The train leaves at 12:51.*
Von welchem Gleis? — *From which platform?*
Vom Gleis 22. — *From platform 22.*
Wann kommt der Zug an? — *When does the train arrive?*
Der Zug kommt um 19:18 Uhr in Berlin an. — *The train arrives in Berlin at 19:18.*

Had a look ☐ Nearly there ☐ Nailed it ☐

Ferienunterkunft — *Holiday accommodation*
das Hotel(s) — *hotel*
das Gasthaus(-häuser) — *guest house, bed and breakfast*
die Ferienwohnung(en) — *holiday apartment*
die Jugendherberge(n) — *youth hostel*
der Campingplatz (-plätze) — *campsite*
Ich möchte ... übernachten. — *I would like to stay ...*
auf diesem Campingplatz — *on this campsite*
in dieser Ferienwohnung — *in this holiday apartment*
in dieser Jugendherberge — *in this youth hostel*
in diesem Hotel / Gasthaus — *in this hotel / guest house*
Es gibt ... — *There is ...*
einen Computerraum — *a computer room*
einen Spieleraum — *a games / play room*
eine gute Aussicht — *a good view*
eine Sauna — *a sauna*
ein Freibad — *an open-air swimming pool*
Er/Sie/Es ist ... — *It is ...*
praktisch — *practical*

Kapitel 5 Wörter

ideal	ideal
laut	noisy
schön	lovely

Had a look ☐ Nearly there ☐ Nailed it ☐

Ich habe (in diesem Hotel) übernachtet.	I stayed (in this hotel).
Das Zimmer war …	The room was …
klein	small
groß	big
(un)bequem	(un)comfortable
schmutzig	dirty
Es gab …	There was …
kein WLAN	no Wi-Fi
viel Lärm	a lot of noise
Es waren Haare in der Dusche.	There were hairs in the shower.
Ich habe eine Maus … gesehen.	I saw a mouse …
unter dem Bett	under the bed
im Restaurant	in the restaurant
Jede Nacht habe ich die Discomusik gehört.	I heard the disco music every night.
Ich werde (nie) wieder hier übernachten.	I will (never) stay here again.

Had a look ☐ Nearly there ☐ Nailed it ☐

Wegbeschreibungen / *Directions*

Entschuldige, bitte. / Entschuldigen Sie, bitte.	Excuse me, please.
Wo ist der/die/das …?	Where is the …?
Wie komme ich zu …?	How do I get to …?
Fahr / Fahren Sie …	Go …
mit dem Bus	by bus
mit der U-Bahn-Linie 1	by underground line 1
Geh / Gehen Sie …	Go …
rechts / links / geradeaus	right / left / straight on
bis (zum Dom) …	until (the cathedral) …
über …	over …
an der Ecke rechts	right at the corner
an der Kreuzung links	left at the crossroads
Nimm / Nehmen Sie …	Take …
die erste / zweite Straße links	the first / second road on the left
Überquer / Überqueren Sie …	Cross …
die Ampel(n)	the traffic lights
die Kreuzung	the crossroads
den Platz	the square
Es ist auf der (rechten) Seite.	It's on the (right).
das Museum (Museen)	museum
das Rathaus(-häuser)	town hall
das Theater(-)	theatre

der Dom	cathedral
der Rathausplatz (–plätze)	town hall square
die Oper(n)	opera house

Had a look ☐ Nearly there ☐ Nailed it ☐

Essen / *Eating*

die Kneipe(n)	pub, bar
das Café(s)	café
das Restaurant(s)	restaurant
der Schnellimbiss(e)	snack bar
die Vorspeise(n)	starter
die Hauptspeise(n)	main course
die Nachspeise(n)	dessert
das Tagesgericht	daily special
die Beilage(n)	side dish
das Getränk(e)	drink
die Champignons	mushrooms
der Gemüsestrudel	vegetable strudel

Had a look ☐ Nearly there ☐ Nailed it ☐

die Kartoffelsuppe	potato soup
der Lammrücken	rump of lamb
die Rindsuppe	consommé, beef soup
das Sauerkraut	sauerkraut, pickled cabbage
der Wurstteller	cold sausage platter
das Wiener Schnitzel	breaded schnitzel, escalope
der Apfelstrudel	apple strudel
die Eissorte	ice cream flavour
die Sachertorte	Sacher torte
das Bier (vom Fass)	(draught) beer
der Fruchtsaft	fruit juice
der Wein	wine

Had a look ☐ Nearly there ☐ Nailed it ☐

Im Restaurant / *In the restaurant*

Wir möchten bitte einen Tisch für vier Personen.	We would like a table for four people.
Der Tisch …	The table …
hat keine Aussicht	doesn't have a view
ist in der Ecke	is in the corner
ist zu klein	is too small
Dieser Löffel ist sehr schmutzig.	This spoon is very dirty.
Es ist ein Haar in diesem Salat.	There is a hair in this salad.
Dieser Wurstteller war sehr fettig.	This sausage platter was very fatty.
Das war …	That was …
unappetitlich	unappetising
zu würzig / salzig	too spicy / salty
Ich möchte mich beschweren.	I would like to complain.

K 5

31

Kapitel 5 Wörter

Ich werde (die Suppe) nicht bezahlen.	I won't pay for (the soup).
Wir werden in ein anderes Restaurant gehen.	We will go to another restaurant.
Ich werde dieses Restaurant nicht empfehlen.	I will not recommend this restaurant.

Had a look ☐ Nearly there ☐ Nailed it ☐

Einkaufen / *Shopping*

der Kuli(s)	ballpoint pen
der Schmuck	jewellery
die Brieftasche(n)	wallet
die Tasse(n)	mug, cup
das Tischtuch(-tücher)	table cloth
die Kekse (pl)	biscuits
der Markt (Märkte)	market
der Souvenirladen (-läden)	souvenir shop
der Andenkenladen (-läden)	souvenir shop
das Kaufhaus(-häuser)	department store
das Einkaufszentrum (-zentren)	shopping centre
Ich suche ein Geschenk.	I'm looking for a present.
Welche Größe?	What size?
klein / mittel / groß	small / medium / large
Welche Farbe mag er?	Which colour does he like?
Seine Lieblingsfarbe ist (rot).	His favourite colour is (red).

Had a look ☐ Nearly there ☐ Nailed it ☐

bunt	multi-coloured
(grün-weiß) gestreift	(green and white) striped
preiswert	inexpensive
teuer	expensive
altmodisch	old-fashioned
beliebt	popular
kaputt	broken
kurz	short
lang	long
schmutzig	dirty
im Sonderangebot	on special offer
… funktioniert nicht	… doesn't work
… hat ein Loch	… has a hole

Had a look ☐ Nearly there ☐ Nailed it ☐

Probleme unterwegs / *Problems out and about*

Mir ist schlecht.	I feel ill.
Mir ist schwindelig.	I feel dizzy.
Mir ist kalt / heiß.	I feel cold / hot.
Der Arm tut mir weh.	My arm hurts.
Mir geht es (nicht) gut.	I'm (not) well.
Ich bin gefallen.	I fell over.
Ich habe meine Schlüssel verloren.	I have lost my keys.
Ich habe kein Geld.	I don't have any money.
Ich möchte einen Handy-Diebstahl melden.	I'd like to report a mobile phone theft.
Sie müssen / Du musst …	You must …
zum Restaurant gehen	go to the restaurant
zum Fundbüro gehen	go to the lost property office
zum Geldautomaten gehen	go to the cash point
zur Polizeiwache gehen	go to the police station
zur Apotheke gehen	go to the chemist's
ins Krankenhaus gehen	go to hospital

Had a look ☐ Nearly there ☐ Nailed it ☐

Kapitel 5 Wörter

Extra words I should know for reading and listening activities

Reisen — *Travelling*
das Boot(e) — boat
die Fähre(n) — ferry
der Reisebus(–busse) — coach
der Bahnsteig(e) — platform
die Haltestelle(n) — stop (bus, tram, etc.)
der Fahrkartenautomat(en) — ticket machine
der Fahrkartenschalter — ticket office
der Hauptbahnhof — main railway station
das Reisebüro(s) — travel agency
der Speisewagen — dining car, restaurant car (on train)
der Wartesaal — waiting room (at station)
das Gepäck — luggage
der Koffer(–) — suitcase
die Reisetasche(n) — travel bag

Had a look ☐ Nearly there ☐ Nailed it ☐

Unterwegs — *On the move*
die Fahrt(en) — journey
der Flug (Flüge) — flight
die Reise(n) — journey
die Richtung(en) — direction
die Ermäßigung(en) — reduction
der Fahrpreis(e) — fare
die Verspätung — delay
aussteigen* — to get off (bus / train)
einsteigen* — to get in/on
umsteigen* — to change (means of transport)
entwerten — to stamp, to validate (a ticket)

Had a look ☐ Nearly there ☐ Nailed it ☐

In der Stadt — *In town*
der/die Besucher(in) — visitor
die Sehenswürdigkeit(en) — tourist attraction, sight
die Busrundfahrt(en) — bus tour
die Führung(en) — guided tour
die Rundfahrt(en) — round trip, tour
der Stadtbummel — stroll through town
die Stadtrundfahrt — sightseeing tour of a town / city
die Öffnungszeiten — opening times
der Stadtplan(–pläne) — town plan / map
die Brücke(n) — bridge
die Burg(en) — (fortified) castle
das Denkmal(e) — monument
der Kirchturm(–türme) — church tower, spire
die Kunstgalerie — art gallery

der Bürgersteig — pavement
der Zebrastreifen — zebra crossing
besichtigen — to sightsee, to visit
sehenswert — worth seeing

Had a look ☐ Nearly there ☐ Nailed it ☐

Essen und trinken — *Eating and drinking*
die Getränkekarte — drinks menu
das Tagesmenü — menu of the day.
das Trinkgeld — tip (for waiter/waitress)
die Eisdiele(n) — ice cream parlour
die Selbstbedienung — self-service
der Speisesaal — dining hall, dining room
die Gabel — fork
das Glas (Gläser) — glass
das Kännchen(–) — pot (tea, coffee)
das Messer — knife
die Tasse(n) — cup
der Teelöffel(–) — teaspoon
der Teller(–) — plate
hausgemacht — home-made
fettig — greasy

Had a look ☐ Nearly there ☐ Nailed it ☐

Einkaufen — *Shopping*
das Geschäft(e) — shop
die Bäckerei — bakery
die Buchhandlung — book shop
die Drogerie — chemist's
das Kaufhaus(–häuser) — department store
die Konditorei — confectioner's
das Lebensmittelgeschäft — grocer's
die Metzgerei — butcher's
die Reinigung — dry cleaner's
das Warenhaus(–häuser) — department store
die Quittung(en) — receipt
die Rolltreppe(n) — escalator
das Schaufenster(–) — shop window
das Sonderangebot(e) — special offer

Had a look ☐ Nearly there ☐ Nailed it ☐

⭐ *Look carefully at small words at the start of verbs which can change their meaning:*

einsteigen to get in/on Ich **steige** in den Bus **ein**.

aussteigen to get out/off Er **steigt** aus dem Zug **aus**.

umsteigen to change (e.g. trains) Wir **steigen** in Köln **um**.

Kapitel 6 Wörter

Words I should know for speaking and writing activities

Himmelsrichtungen	Points of the compass
der Kompass	compass
der Norden	north
der Nordosten	north east
der Osten	east
der Südosten	south east
der Süden	south
der Südwesten	south west
der Westen	west
der Nordwesten	north west
im Norden	in the north
im Osten	in the east
im Süden	in the south
im Westen	in the west
in der Mitte	in the middle

Had a look ☐ Nearly there ☐ Nailed it ☐

Länder und Orte	Countries and places
das Reiseziel	travel destination
das Urlaubsziel	holiday destination
im Ausland	abroad
im Inland	at home, inland
Europa	Europe
Bayern	Bavaria
die Nordsee	the North Sea
die Ostsee	the Baltic Sea
Spanien	Spain
Kroatien	Croatia
Italien	Italy
Österreich	Austria
die Türkei	Turkey

Had a look ☐ Nearly there ☐ Nailed it ☐

Ich fahre …	I am going …
nach Spanien	to Spain
nach Italien	to Italy
in die Türkei	to Turkey
ans Meer	to the sea
an einen See	to a lake
an den Strand	to the beach
an die Küste	to the coast
in den Wald	to a forest
in die Berge	to the mountains

Had a look ☐ Nearly there ☐ Nailed it ☐

Das Wetter	The weather
der Frost	frost
das Gewitter	thunderstorm
der Hagel	hail
der Nebel	fog
der Regen	rain
der Schnee	snow
die Sonne	sun
der Wind	wind
die Wolken (pl)	clouds

Had a look ☐ Nearly there ☐ Nailed it ☐

Es ist …	It is …
frostig	frosty
heiß	hot
kalt	cold
neblig	foggy
sonnig	sunny
windig	windy
wolkig	cloudy
Es …	It is …
friert	freezing
hagelt	hailing
regnet	raining
schneit	snowing

Had a look ☐ Nearly there ☐ Nailed it ☐

Es gibt …	There is / are …
Nebel	fog
ein Gewitter	a thunderstorm
Wolken	clouds
Es wird (heiß) sein.	It will be (hot).
Es wird hageln.	It will hail.
Es wird regnen.	It will rain.
Es wird schneien.	It will snow.
Es wird ein Gewitter geben.	There will be a thunderstorm.
Die Temperatur wird (11) Grad sein.	The temperature will be (11) degrees.

Had a look ☐ Nearly there ☐ Nailed it ☐

die Jahreszeit	season
meine Lieblingsjahreszeit	my favourite season
der Frühling	spring
der Sommer	summer
der Herbst	autumn
der Winter	winter
Die Nächte werden kalt.	The nights become / are becoming cold.
Die Tage werden länger.	The days become / are becoming longer.
Die Tage werden kürzer.	The days become / are becoming shorter.
Das Wetter wird besser.	The weather becomes / is becoming better.

Had a look ☐ Nearly there ☐ Nailed it ☐

Kapitel 6 Wörter

Urlaubsarten	Types of holidays
Ich mache (nicht) gern ...	I (don't) like going on a/an ...
Abenteuerurlaub	adventure holiday
Aktivurlaub	active holiday
Sightseeingurlaub	sightseeing holiday
Sommerurlaub	summer holiday
Strandurlaub	beach holiday
Urlaub auf Balkonien	staycation / holiday at home
Winterurlaub	winter holiday
Ich gehe (nicht) gern zelten.	I (don't) like going camping.
Ich gehe (nicht) gern ..., weil ich ...	I (don't) like going ... because I ...
abenteuerlustig bin	am adventurous
sportlich bin	am sporty
aktiv bin	am active
gern schwimme	like swimming
gern in der Sonne liege	like sunbathing
gern draußen bin	like being outdoors
gern Zeit mit Familie verbringe	enjoy spending time with family
gern Zeit mit Freunden verbringe	enjoy spending time with friends
mich schnell langweile	get bored easily
nichts tun will	don't want to do anything

Had a look ☐ Nearly there ☐ Nailed it ☐

Urlaubsaktivitäten	Holiday activities
während des Urlaubs	during the holiday
außerhalb der Stadt	outside the town
innerhalb der Stadt	inside the town
wegen des Wetters	because of the weather
trotz der Touristen	despite the tourists
eine neue / aufregende Aktivität	a new / exciting activity
Achterbahn fahren	to go on a rollercoaster
Wanderungen machen	to go hiking
Fahrräder mieten	to rent / hire bicycles
eine Raftingtour machen	to go on a rafting trip
eine Canyoningtour machen	to go on a canyoning trip
die Übernachtung	overnight stay
im Zelt übernachten	to spend the night in a tent
in einer Hütte übernachten	to spend the night in a hut / cabin
im Luxushotel übernachten	to spend the night in a luxury hotel
Vollpension	full board
Halbpension	half board
das Zweibettzimmer	twin room

Had a look ☐ Nearly there ☐ Nailed it ☐

In der Stadt	In town
Es gibt ...	There is ...
eine Autobahn	a motorway
einen Bahnhof	a station
einen Campingplatz	a campsite
ein Eiscafé	an ice cream café
ein Freibad	an open-air pool
ein Fußballstadion	a football stadium
eine Fußgängerzone	a pedestrianised area
eine Grundschule	a primary school
einen Kindergarten	a nursery
eine Schule	a school

Had a look ☐ Nearly there ☐ Nailed it ☐

Es gibt ...	There are ...
viele Touristen	lots of tourists
viele Geschäfte	lots of shops
viele Sehenswürdigkeiten	lots of sights
gute Restaurants	good restaurants
viele Vorteile	lots of advantages
viele Nachteile	lots of disadvantages
Es gibt ...	There is ...
keinen Flughafen	no airport
keine Universität	no university
kein Kino	no cinema
Es gibt keine Strände.	There are no beaches.

Had a look ☐ Nearly there ☐ Nailed it ☐

Meine Stadt: Vor- und Nachteile	My town: advantages and disadvantages
Ich wohne ...	I live ...
auf einem Bauernhof	on a farm
auf dem Land	in the countryside
in einem Dorf	in a village
in einer Kleinstadt	in a small town
in einer Großstadt	in a city
in einer Hauptstadt	in a capital city
in der Nähe von ...	near ...
Es gibt ...	There is ...
viel zu tun	a lot to do
viel Lärm	a lot of noise
viel Verkehr	a lot of traffic
Es gibt nicht viele Autos.	There aren't many cars.
Es gibt nicht viel für Jugendliche zu tun.	There's not much for young people to do.
Es gibt keine Buslinie.	There is no bus route.

Had a look ☐ Nearly there ☐ Nailed it ☐

Es gab ...	There was ...
einen tollen Park	a great park
ein modernes Sportzentrum	a modern sports centre

K 6

35

Kapitel 6 Wörter

Es gab keine großen Diskos.	There were no big discos.
Es wird keine neue Industrie geben.	There will not be any new industry.
Es wird ein Fußballstadion geben.	There will be a football stadium.
Man sollte …	We should …
mehr Busse haben	have more buses
moderne Sportanlagen haben	have modern sports facilities
mehr Aktivitäten für Jugendliche haben	have more activities for young people
Parkplätze am Stadtrand bauen	build car parks on the outskirts of town
die öffentlichen Verkehrsmittel verbessern	improve public transport
mehr Fahrradwege haben	have more cycle paths
Autos in der Innenstadt verbieten	ban cars from the town centre
die Straßen sauber halten	keep the roads clean
Der Vorteil / Nachteil ist …	The advantage / disadvantage is …
Ein großer Vorteil / Nachteil ist …	A big advantage / disadvantage is …
Es gibt viele Vorteile / Nachteile.	There are lots of advantages / disadvantages.

Had a look ☐ **Nearly there** ☐ **Nailed it** ☐

Kapitel 6 Wörter

Extra words I should know for reading and listening activities

Die Natur — *Nature*
das Festland	mainland
die Insel(n)	island
die Küste	coast
das Meer(e)*	sea
das Mittelmeer	Mediterranean Sea
der See(n)*	lake
die See(n)*	sea
der Wald (Wälder)	wood, forest
die Wiese(n)	meadow
der Himmel	sky
die Landschaft	landscape
der Baum (Bäume)	tree
das Blatt (Blätter)	leaf (on tree or other plant)

Had a look ☐ Nearly there ☐ Nailed it ☐

Meine Gegend — *My area*
der Badeort(e)**	seaside resort
das Bauernhaus (–häuser)	farm house
das Gebäude(–)	building
der Einwohner(–)	inhabitant
der Hafen (Häfen)	harbour, port
der Stau(s)	traffic jam
der Supermarkt (–märkte)	supermarket
die Umgebung(en)	surrounding area
die Verbindung(en)	(transport) connection
anbieten	to offer
kontrollieren	to control

Had a look ☐ Nearly there ☐ Nailed it ☐

Im Urlaub — *On holiday*
der Badeanzug	swimsuit
die Badehose	swimming trunks
der Blick(e)	view, glance
die Erinnerung(en)	memory
das Plakat(e)	poster, billboard
das Formular(e)	form
die Pension(en)	bed and breakfast, guesthouse, (small) hotel
der Wohnwagen**	caravan
das Zelt(e)	tent
die Landkarte(n)	map
die Straßenkarte(n)	road map
das Schließfach (–fächer)	locker
der Sicherheitsgurt(e)	safety belt, seat belt
die Überfahrt(en)	crossing (sea)
erleben	to experience
zelten	to camp
seekrank*	seasick

Had a look ☐ Nearly there ☐ Nailed it ☐

Urlaubsaktivitäten — *Holiday activities*
die Fahrradvermietung	bicycle hire
der Fotoapparat(e)	camera
das Segelboot(e)	sailing boat
der Sonnenbrand	sunburn
die Sonnencreme	suntan lotion
der Strandkorb (–körbe)	wicker beach chair with a hood
der Yogakurs(e)	yoga course
(sich) sonnen	to sunbathe
windsurfen	to windsurf

Had a look ☐ Nearly there ☐ Nailed it ☐

⭐ *There are two words for 'sea' in German, das Meer and die See:*

Ich fahre ans Meer / an die See.
I'm going to the seaside.

Das Meer / Die See war sehr kalt.
The sea was very cold.

Note that See is often used in compound nouns:

der Seeblick sea view

seekrank seasick

Look carefully at the gender to distinguish between 'sea' (die See) and 'lake' (der See).

⭐ **To work out the meaning of a new word, ask yourself if it is similar to one you already know, and if it contains cognates or near-cognates:

der Wohnwagen → wohnen (to live) + Wagen (car / van) = literally 'living van', or 'caravan'

der Badeort → baden (to swim / to bathe) + Ort (place) = literally 'swimming place', or 'seaside resort'

Remember to think beyond the literal translation when working out the correct English meaning.

Words I should know for speaking and writing activities

Berufe — Jobs

der/die Apotheker(in)	chemist
der/die Architekt(in)	architect
der/die Arzt/Ärztin	doctor
der/die Bäcker(in)	baker
der/die Beamte/Beamtin	civil servant
der/die Bibliothekar(in)	librarian
der/die Elektriker(in)	electrician
der/die Fahrer(in)	driver
der/die Feuerwehrmann/-frau	firefighter
der/die Freiwillige	volunteer
der/die Friseur/Friseuse	hairdresser
der/die Informatiker(in)	computer scientist
der/die Journalist(in)	journalist
der/die Kellner(in)	waiter/waitress
der/die Klempner(in)	plumber
der/die Koch/Köchin	cook
der/die Krankenpfleger/Krankenschwester	nurse

Had a look ☐   Nearly there ☐   Nailed it ☐

der/die Lehrer(in)	teacher
der/die Manager(in)	manager
der/die Mechaniker(in)	mechanic
der/die Metzger(in)	butcher
der/die Pilot(in)	pilot
der/die Programmierer(in)	computer programmer
der/die Schauspieler(in)	actor/actress
der/die Sozialarbeiter(in)	social worker
der/die Tierarzt/Tierärztin	vet
der/die Verkäufer(in)	sales assistant
der/die Übersetzer(in)	translator
der/die Zahnarzt/Zahnärztin	dentist

Had a look ☐   Nearly there ☐   Nailed it ☐

Arbeitsorte — Places of work

der Keller(–)	cellar
der Laden (Läden)	shop
die Apotheke(n)	chemist's
die Autowerkstatt (–stätten)	garage
die Bäckerei(en)	bakery
die Bank(en)	bank
die Metzgerei(en)	butcher's
das Büro(s)	office
das Geschäft(e)	shop
der Supermarkt (–märkte)	supermarket
das Krankenhaus (–häuser)	hospital
das Altenheim(e)	elderly care home
das Labor(s)	laboratory
das Reisebüro(s)	travel agency
das Restaurant(s)	restaurant
die Schule(n)	school
das Theater(–)	theatre
die Tierklinik(en)	animal surgery

Had a look ☐   Nearly there ☐   Nailed it ☐

Berufsbilder — Job descriptions

Er/Sie hat ausgezeichnete … Deutschkenntnisse	He/She has an excellent … knowledge of German
Sprachkenntnisse	knowledge of languages
Er/Sie ist in (Deutsch) fließend.	He/She is fluent in (German).
Er/Sie kann gut kommunizieren.	He/She can communicate well.
Er/Sie interessiert sich für die technischen Aspekte.	He/She is interested in the technical aspects.
Er/Sie …	He/She …
schreibt Reportagen	writes reports
berichtet über aktuelle Themen	reports on current issues
macht Interviews mit Stars	interviews stars
ist zuverlässig	is reliable
ist pünktlich	is punctual

Had a look ☐   Nearly there ☐   Nailed it ☐

Er/Sie hat eine gute Ausbildung.	He/She has a good education.
Ein Hochschulabschluss / Praktikum ist nicht notwendig.	A degree / work experience is not necessary.
Das Gehalt ist niedrig / großzügig.	The salary is low / generous.
Er/Sie arbeitet …	He/She works …
bei einer Firma	for a company
in einem Geschäft	in a shop
in einem Altenheim	in an elderly care home
in einem Krankenhaus	in a hospital

Kapitel 7 Wörter

in privaten Häusern	in private houses
zuerst	first, firstly
danach	after that
dann	then
schließlich	finally

Had a look ☐ Nearly there ☐ Nailed it ☐

Berufsprofile — Job profiles

Ich interessiere mich für den Job als …,	I'm interested in the job as …
weil …	because …
ich (in Mathe) begabt bin	I'm good at / gifted in (maths)
ich (in der Touristik) arbeiten möchte	I would like to work in (tourism)
Seit drei Jahren …	For three years …
bin ich Mitglied im Orchester	I have been a member of an orchestra
bin ich Kapitän der (Handball-)Mannschaft	I have been captain of the (handball) team
gehe ich zum Sportverein	I have been going to a sports club
Ich bekomme gute Noten.	I get good grades.
Meine Noten sind nicht so gut.	My grades are not so good.
Meine Durchschnittsnote ist …	My average grade is …
Ich habe einen Teilzeitjob als (Touristenführer(in)).	I have a part-time job as a (tour guide).
Ich habe einen Ferienjob als …	I have a holiday job as a …
Letzten Sommer habe ich als (Freiwillige(r)) gearbeitet.	Last summer I worked as (a volunteer).

Had a look ☐ Nearly there ☐ Nailed it ☐

Ich bin …	I am …
kreativ	creative
geduldig	patient
fleißig	hard-working
pünktlich	punctual
Ich konzentriere mich auf den Schulunterricht.	I concentrate on school lessons.
Ich interessiere mich für (das Skifahren).	I am interested in (skiing).
Ich nehme an der (Mathe-Olympiade) teil.	I take part in (the maths olympics).
Ich hoffe auf eine Karriere (in der Touristik).	I am hoping for a career (in tourism).
Ich freue mich auf …	I am looking forward to …

Had a look ☐ Nearly there ☐ Nailed it ☐

Mein Lebenslauf — My CV

die Schulbildung	school education
der Schulabschluss	school-leaving qualification
der Schulerfolg	school achievement / success
der Hochschulabschluss	degree
die Arbeitserfahrung	work experience
das Hobby(s)	hobby
das Interesse(n)	interest

Had a look ☐ Nearly there ☐ Nailed it ☐

Traumberufe — Dream jobs

Als Kind wollte ich (Feuerwehrmann / Clown) werden.	As a child, I wanted to become (a firefighter / a clown).
Ich interessiere mich nicht mehr für …	I am no longer interested in …
Ich möchte … arbeiten.	I would like to work …
als (Manager(in))	as a (manager)
im Ausland	abroad
in (den USA)	in (the USA)
freiwillig	voluntarily
bei einer (internationalen) Firma	for an (international) company
beim Zirkus	for a circus
Ich möchte …	I would like …
in einer Hütte in den Alpen wohnen	to live in a hut / cabin in the Alps
nach (Thailand) reisen	to travel to (Thailand)
ein Jahr in (Thailand) verbringen	to spend a year in (Thailand)
eine Lehre machen	to do an apprenticeship
Marketing machen	to do marketing
Ich habe das Abitur (nicht) bestanden.	I passed (did not pass) my A levels.

Had a look ☐ Nearly there ☐ Nailed it ☐

Sprachen öffnen Türen — Languages open doors

Im Moment lerne ich (Mandarin), um …	At the moment I'm learning (Mandarin) in order to …
Ich möchte (Griechisch) lernen, um …	I would like to learn (Greek) in order to …
mich um einen guten Job zu bewerben	apply for a good job
(in China) zu arbeiten	work (in China)
meine (Deutsch-)Kenntnisse zu verbessern	improve my knowledge of (German)
die Leute besser kennenzulernen	get to know the people better
die Kultur besser kennenzulernen	get to know the culture better

K 7

Kapitel 7 Wörter

die Sprache besser kennenzulernen	*get to know the language better*
(die Opern) richtig zu verstehen	*understand (the operas) properly*
durch das Land zu reisen	*travel around the country*
mit Leuten in ihrer Muttersprache zu kommunizieren	*communicate with people in their native language*
nach (Spanien) auszuwandern	*emigrate to (Spain)*
mich zu amüsieren	*have fun*
Im Moment lerne ich (Mandarin), weil es … ist.	*At the moment I'm learning (Mandarin) because it is …*
Pflichtfach	*a compulsory subject*
nötig / notwendig	*necessary, essential*
wichtig	*important*

Had a look ☐ **Nearly there** ☐ **Nailed it** ☐

Extra words I should know for reading and listening activities

Berufe — *Jobs*
der/die Angestellte	*employee*
der/die Besitzer(in)	*owner*
der/die Chef(in)	*boss*
der/die Kollege/Kollegin	*colleague*
der/die Mitarbeiter(in)	*employee, colleague*
der/die Bauer/Bäuerin*	*farmer*
der/die Bauarbeiter(in)*	*building / construction worker*
der/die Briefträger(in)	*postman/woman*
der/die Fleischer(in)	*butcher*
der/die Fremd-sprachenassistent(in)	*foreign language assistant*
der/die Gärtner(in)	*gardener*
die Hausfrau	*house wife*
der Hausmann	*house husband*
der/die Kassierer(in)	*cashier, bank clerk*
der/die LKW-Fahrer(in)	*lorry driver*
der/die Maler(in)	*painter, decorator*
der/die Pfarrer(in)	*parish priest, vicar*
der/die Postbote/Postbotin	*postman/woman*
der/die Rentner(in)	*pensioner*
der/die Tischler(in)	*carpenter*

Had a look ☐ Nearly there ☐ Nailed it ☐

Bei der Arbeit — *At work*
der Bauernhof*	*farm*
die Baustelle*	*building site*
das Büro(s)	*office*
der Friseursalon(s)	*hairdresser's*
im Freien	*outside, in the open air*
der Hausbau	*house building / construction*
der/die Kunde/Kundin	*customer*
die Arbeitszeit	*work hours (pl)*
die Bezahlung(en)	*payment*
der Lohn (Löhne)	*wage*
der Mindestlohn	*minimum wage*
die Stelle(n)	*job*
die Halbtagsarbeit	*part-time / half-day work*
die Schichtarbeit	*shift work*
die Vollzeitarbeit	*full-time work*
gut / schlecht bezahlt	*well / badly paid*
ganztags	*all day*
berufstätig (sein)	*(to be) in work*
anbauen*	*to grow (crops)*
bauen*	*to build*
besitzen	*to own*

Had a look ☐ Nearly there ☐ Nailed it ☐

Studium und Ausbildung — *Studies and training*
der/die Abiturient(in)	*person doing the Abitur*
der Sprachkurs(e)	*language course*
der Sprachunterricht	*language classes*
der Studienplatz (–plätze)	*university place*
die Wirtschaft	*economics (subject)*
der Nebenjob(s)	*part-time job*
das Semester(–)	*term*
das Taschengeld	*pocket money*
theoretisch	*theoretical*
der/die Auszubildende (Azubi)	*apprentice, trainee*
der Ausbildungsplatz (–plätze)	*vacancy / place for a trainee*
der/die Berufsberater(in)	*careers adviser*
die Berufsschule(n)	*vocational training school*
der Rat	*advice*

Had a look ☐ Nearly there ☐ Nailed it ☐

Bewerbungen — *Job applications*
die Bewerbung(en)	*application*
der Brief(e)	*letter*
der Termin(e)	*date, appointment*
das Vorstellungsgespräch(e)	*job interview*
der Wunsch (Wünsche)	*wish*
die Gelegenheit(en)	*opportunity*
der Führerschein	*driving licence*

Had a look ☐ Nearly there ☐ Nailed it ☐

⭐ *Look out for word families when working out the meaning of words, but remember to use the context of the text to help you too.*

Bauen means 'to build' and *anbauen* means 'to grow' and you have come across several words using the stem *bau*:

Der Bauer and *der Bauarbeiter* both look similar, but one means 'farmer' and the other 'builder'.

Der Bauernhof and *die Baustelle* also look quite similar, but which is a 'farm', and which a 'building site'?

Using the language around the words will help you work out the meaning:

Ich wohne auf einem Bauernhof auf dem Land.
I live on a farm in the countryside.

Here, the verb *wohne* and the location *auf dem Land* help you decide that *Bauernhof* must be a farm rather than a building site.

Words I should know for speaking and writing activities

Festivals und Events — *Festivals and events*

Mein Lieblingsmusikfestival ist …	My favourite music festival is …
Mein Lieblingsevent ist …	My favourite event is …
die Pariser Modewoche	Paris fashion week
der Eurovision Song Contest	the Eurovision Song Contest
die Fußballweltmeisterschaft	the football World Cup
Mein Lieblingsevent sind …	My favourite event is …
die Filmfestspiele von Cannes	the Cannes Film Festival
die Olympischen Winterspiele	the Winter Olympic Games
die Olympischen Sommerspiele	the Summer Olympic Games
Das Festival / Event findet … statt.	The festival / event takes place …
in Deutschland / England	in Germany / England
jeden Sommer / Winter	every summer / winter
jedes Jahr	every year
alle vier Jahre	every four years
Ich habe … gesehen / besucht.	I saw / visited …
Das Festival war …	The festival was …
sehr interessant / langweilig	very interesting / boring
total spannend / toll	totally exciting / great
ziemlich laut	quite loud

Had a look ☐ Nearly there ☐ Nailed it ☐

Ein sportliches Event — *A sporting event*

der Informationskiosk	information stand
die Ziellinie	finish line
das Souvenirgeschäft	souvenir shop
der Massageraum	massage room
die Kleiderabgabe	cloakroom
die Kinderkrippe	crèche
Auf dem Foto sind …	In the photo are …
zwei Personen	two people
drei Athleten	three athletes
Die Personen …	The people …
Die Athleten …	The athletes …
laufen um das Stadtzentrum	are running around the town centre
skaten durch die Stadt	are skating through the town
spielen bei der Fußballweltmeisterschaft	are playing at the football World Cup
nehmen an den Olympischen Spielen / an einem sportlichen Event teil	are taking part in the Olympic Games / a sporting event

Had a look ☐ Nearly there ☐ Nailed it ☐

Man kann viele … sehen.	You can see lots of …
Athleten	athletes
Teilnehmer	participants
Zuschauer	spectators
Ich finde, Sport macht Spaß, weil …	I find sport fun because …
Ich finde, Sport macht keinen Spaß, weil …	I don't find sport fun because …
Sport gut für die Fitness ist	sport is good for fitness
ich sportlich / aktiv bin	I am sporty / active
ich nicht sportlich / aktiv bin	I am not sporty / active
Ich will am Marathon / an den Olympischen Spielen / an der Fußballweltmeisterschaft teilnehmen, denn …	I want to take part in the marathon / Olympic Games / football World Cup because …
ich interessiere mich für …	I'm interested in …
mein Lieblingshobby ist …	my favourite hobby is …
ich möchte eine Medaille gewinnen	I would like to win a medal

Had a look ☐ Nearly there ☐ Nailed it ☐

Die Olympischen Winterspiele — *The Winter Olympics*

Im Jahr (1976) haben die Olympischen Spiele in … stattgefunden.	In (1976) the Olympic Games took place in …
eine Bronzemedaille	a bronze medal
eine Silbermedaille	a silver medal
eine Goldmedaille	a gold medal
Die Athleten haben … Medaillen gewonnen.	The athletes won … medals.
die Baustelle(n)	building / construction works
die Gastgeberstadt (-städte)	host city
die Luftverschmutzung	air pollution
der Stau(s)	traffic jam
die Sprache	language
die Kultur(en)	culture
der Tourist(en)	tourist
der Zeitdruck	time pressure
der Unfall(-fälle)	accident
die Infrastruktur	infrastructure
schmutzig	dirty
unsicher	unsafe
der Einwohner(–)	resident

Had a look ☐ Nearly there ☐ Nailed it ☐

Kapitel 8 Wörter

Eine Debatte	A debate
Meiner Meinung nach sind die Olympischen Spiele gut / nicht gut, weil …	In my opinion, the Olympic Games are good / not good because …
Ich finde, die Olympischen Spiele sind wichtig / nicht wichtig, weil …	I find the Olympic Games are important / not important because …
Auf der einen Seite …	On the one hand …
Auf der anderen Seite …	On the other hand …
Einerseits …	On the one hand …
Andererseits …	On the other hand …
Ich stimme zu.	I agree.
Ich stimme da nicht zu.	I don't agree.
Vielleicht …, aber …	Perhaps … but …

Had a look ☐ Nearly there ☐ Nailed it ☐

Die Länder	Countries
Albanien	Albania
Armenien	Armenia
Australien	Australia
Belgien	Belgium
Deutschland	Germany
Estland	Estonia
Frankreich	France
Georgien	Georgia
Griechenland	Greece
Großbritannien	Great Britain
Israel	Israel
Italien	Italy
Lettland	Latvia
Litauen	Lithuania
Luxemburg	Luxembourg
Montenegro	Montenegro
Norwegen	Norway
die Niederlande	the Netherlands

Had a look ☐ Nearly there ☐ Nailed it ☐

Österreich	Austria
Polen	Poland
Rumänien	Romania
Russland	Russia
Schweden	Sweden
die Schweiz	Switzerland
Serbien	Serbia
Slowenien	Slovenia
Spanien	Spain
Ungarn	Hungary
Zypern	Cyprus

Had a look ☐ Nearly there ☐ Nailed it ☐

Der Eurovision Song Contest	The Eurovision Song Contest
der Deutsche / die Deutsche	the German person
ein Deutscher / eine Deutsche	a German person
das Interessante	the interesting thing
das Gute	the good thing
etwas Interessantes	something interesting
nichts Interessantes	nothing interesting
viel Gutes	much good
wenig Gutes	little good
Ich interessiere mich für den Eurovision Song Contest, weil …	I'm interested in the Eurovision Song Contest because …
Für mich sind die Vorteile …	The advantages for me are …
Ich finde, die Nachteile sind …	I find the disadvantages are …
Ich will am Contest teilnehmen, weil …	I want to take part in the Contest because …
Ich will nicht am Contest teilnehmen, weil …	I don't want to take part in the Contest because …
der Contest europäische Nationen zusammen bringt	the Contest brings European nations together
der Contest sehr teuer ist	the Contest is very expensive
es oft politische Probleme gibt	there are often political problems
es oft viele Nachteile für das Gastgeberland gibt	there are often many problems for the host country

Had a look ☐ Nearly there ☐ Nailed it ☐

Umwelt macht Schule	Setting environmental standards at school
der Umweltschutz	environmental protection
die Umweltaktion	environmental action
Man sollte …	We should …
eine Solaranlage installieren	install solar panels
den Müll trennen	sort the rubbish
Druckerpatronen / Kopierkartuschen recyceln	recycle printer / copier cartridges
eine Fahrradwoche organisieren	organise a bike week
Energie sparen	save energy
Nistkästen für Vögel bauen	build bird boxes

K 8

Kapitel 8 Wörter

Obst und Gemüse kompostieren	compost fruit and vegetables
Bienenvölker im Schulgarten halten	keep beehives in the school garden
effektiver recyceln	recycle more effectively
oft	often
leicht	easy
effektiv	effective
schnell	quick
bestimmt	definitely
vielleicht	maybe
nie	never

Had a look ☐ **Nearly there** ☐ **Nailed it** ☐

Wie werden wir „grüner"?
How do we become 'greener'?

die Dürre	drought
die Luftverschmutzung	air pollution
der saure Regen	acid rain
die Wasserverschmutzung	water pollution
die globale Erwärmung	global warming
die Abholzung	deforestation
das Aussterben von Tierarten	the extinction of animal species
vom Aussterben bedroht	threatened with extinction
die Gletscher schmelzen	the glaciers are melting
Das ist ein großes Problem, weil …	It's a big problem because …
Das größte Problem ist …	The biggest problem is …
Man sollte …	We should …
die Tiere schützen	protect animals
die Wälder nicht zerstören	not destroy forests
mehr Bäume pflanzen	plant more trees
weniger Bäume fällen	cut down fewer trees
weniger abholzen	deforest less

Had a look ☐ **Nearly there** ☐ **Nailed it** ☐

Kampagnen und gute Zwecke
Campaigns and good causes

Ich will …	I want to …
mit blinden Kindern arbeiten	work with blind children
in einer Schule unterrichten	teach in a school
bei einer Schutzorganisation arbeiten	work for a protection organisation
bei einer Umweltschutzorganisation arbeiten	work for an environmental protection organisation
bei einer Hilfsorganisation arbeiten	work for an aid organisation
Fußball mit armen Kindern spielen	play football with poor children
freiwillig arbeiten	work as a volunteer
der Natur helfen	help nature
der Umwelt helfen	help the environment
Kindern helfen	help children
armen Menschen helfen	help poor people
ein Projekt im Ausland machen	do a project abroad
Straßenkinder	street children
die Partnerschule	partner school

Had a look ☐ **Nearly there** ☐ **Nailed it** ☐

Kapitel 8 Wörter

Extra words I should know for reading and listening activities

Festivals und Events	*Festivals and events*
die Ausstellung(en)	exhibition
die Diskussion(en)	discussion
der Marathon(s)	marathon
die Modenschau(en)	fashion show
der Vortag(-träge)	lecture
der Informationskiosk(e)	information desk
das Jugendorchester(-)	youth orchestra
der/die Komponist(in)	composer
die Kapzität	capacity (venue)

Had a look ☐ Nearly there ☐ Nailed it ☐

Umweltprobleme / *Environmental problems*

der Abfall (Abfälle)	rubbish, waste
der Abfalleimer(-)	rubbish bin, litter bin
das Altpapier	waste paper
die Mülltonne(n)	dustbin
die Abgase (pl)	exhaust fumes
das Benzin	petrol
der Brennstoff	fuel
das Gebrauch	usage
der Verbrauch	consumption
verschmutzen	to pollute
das Kraftwerk*	power station
die Kohle	coal
der Treibhauseffekt	greenhouse effect
das Ozonloch	hole in the ozone layer
die Ozonschicht	ozone layer
der saure Regen	acid rain
der Sauerstoff	oxygen
zerstören	to destroy
der Schaden	damage
umweltfeindlich	environmentally unfriendly

Had a look ☐ Nearly there ☐ Nailed it ☐

Wie werden wir „grüner"? / *How do we become 'greener'?*

der Biomüll	organic waste
das Glas	glass
das Metall	metal
das Plastik	plastic
die Plastikflasche(n)	plastic bottle
die Verpackung	packaging
die Unterrichtsstunde(n)	lesson
die Luft (Lüfte)	air
atmen	to breathe
das Licht(er)	light
das Gerät(e)	machine, appliance
ausschalten	to turn off (light, power)
die Raumtemperatur(en)	room temperature
die Regierung(en)	government

der/die Umweltsprecher(in)	environmental representative
die alternative Energiequelle	alternative source of energy
die Sonnenenergie	solar energy
die Wasserkraft	hydroelectric power
biologisch (Bio–)	biological, organic
bleifrei	lead-free

Had a look ☐ Nearly there ☐ Nailed it ☐

Kampagnen und gute Zwecke / *Campaigns and good causes*

die Ernährung	food, nourishment, nutrition
die Gesellschaft	society
fairer Handel	fair trade
die Krankheit(en)	illness
das Menschenrecht(e)	human right
das Tierheim(e)	animal shelter
die Wellblechhütte(n)	corrugated-iron hut
die Wohltätigkeit(en)	charity
das Wohltätigkeitskonzert(e)	charity concert
der Wohltätigkeitsverein(e)	charity
die Wohltätigkeitsveranstaltung(en)	charity event
freiwillig	voluntary
lohnenswert	worthwhile
menschlich	human, humane
überbevölkert	overpopulated
spenden	to donate

Had a look ☐ Nearly there ☐ Nailed it ☐

⭐ *German words don't always translate directly into English. Sometimes you will need to take the sense of a German word and think a bit more broadly to come up with the correct English translation:*

das Kraftwerk → Kraft (power) + Werk (works) = 'power station' rather than 'power works'

K 8

45

ISBN 978-1-292-17255-2